THE OX-HERDER AND THE GOOD SHEPHERD

The Ox-Herder and the Good Shepherd

FINDING CHRIST
ON THE BUDDHA'S PATH

Addison Hodges Hart

William B. Eerdmans Publishing Company
Grand Rapids, Michigan / Cambridge, U.K.

Published 2013 by
Wm. B. Eerdmans Publishing Co.
2140 Oak Industrial Drive N.E., Grand Rapids, Michigan 49505 /
P.O. Box 163, Cambridge CB3 9PU U.K.
www.eerdmans.com

Printed in the United States of America

18 17 16 15 14 13   7 6 5 4 3 2 1

Library of Congress Cataloging-in-Publication Data

Hart, Addison Hodges, 1956-
The Ox-Herder and the Good Shepherd: Finding Christ on
the Buddha's Path / Addison Hodges Hart.
pages   cm
Includes bibliographical references.
ISBN 978-0-8028-6758-2 (pbk.: alk. paper)
1. Jesus Christ — Buddhist interpretations. 2. Kuo'an, 12th cent.
Shi niu tu song. 3. Christianity and other religions — Zen Buddhism.
4. Zen Buddhism — Relations — Christianity. I. Title.

BT304.914H37 2013

294.3'35 — dc23

2013009743

Unless otherwise noted, the Scripture quotations in this publication are
from the Revised Standard Version of the Bible, copyrighted 1946, 1952
© 1971, 1973 by the Division of Christian Education of the National
Council of Churches of Christ in the U.S.A., and used by permission.

For

SISTER CATHERINE GRACE OF ALL SAINTS,

my first teacher in contemplative prayer

Contents

CHAPTER I

Preliminary Remarks: Why a Christian Would Seek a Zen Buddhist Ox

The Christian by definition is someone who is interiorly free.

That is to say, he or she is free to search out everything that leads towards the truth — whether it's the truth about the source and sustainer of all being which we call God and have seen revealed in Jesus Christ, or the truths about this impermanent world and the unfolding creation, or the truths we find within our selves — truths both good and not so good.

Wherever truth is to be found, we are free to search for it.

A Christian should never be fearful of the location of truth. Even when it's in other faiths, other philosophies, history, or science, it's still truth; and if it's true, it is to be trusted. All truth is God's. There can't be anything alien or threatening in it. The Christian who dreads the discovery of any truth, no matter where it's found and even if it overturns cherished presuppositions, or who denies that truth is everywhere and always present, fundamentally denies that God is the one "in [whom] we live and move and have our being," and that all human beings of every time and place are "indeed his offspring" (Acts 17:28). The Christian may seek to make Christ better known wherever he or she is (which is always best served by actions and attitudes, not by arguments and aggressiveness), but no Christian is free to deny the traces of truth that often lie right underfoot.

Not only is the Christian free to seek truth outside the confines of Bible and church (not that there really is an "outside," since all truths are really already "in God"), but the Christian can even draw on the various sources of wisdom that have flowed into and through human minds universally. An old, frequently forgotten Christian principle has been that we should not fear to bring the riches of perennial wisdom *into* the church. Thoughtful Christians have always recognized that the *logos* — meaning "word," "reason," and "message" — was revealed before Jesus embodied it in himself. It was synonymous with the common universal wisdom traceable throughout the history of the race and present in every human culture. The great Latin church father Augustine, for example, wrote in his *Retractions* (I.13.3) that "that which today is called the Christian religion existed among the ancients, and has never ceased to exist from the origin of the human race, until the time when Christ himself came, and men began to call 'Christian' the true religion which already existed beforehand." For Augustine, as for all the greatest Christian thinkers down the ages, wisdom is tapped from many living veins — and it has run through the ages of humankind like the blood that circulates in the human body or like the rivers that flow on the earth and sustain life. The essence of the perennial *logos* of God has given spiritual life and health to the human intellect since its inception.

When Christians become nervous about protecting the "uniqueness" of Christianity among the world's religions, they need to pause and consider that it isn't "uniqueness" at all that they wish to protect. It's the *superiority* of Christianity they really want to assert, and that's quite another matter. After all, everything, and certainly every form of belief, is unique. Buddhism, for instance, is every bit as unique as Christianity, and Buddha is every bit as unique as Christ. The real issue for Christians is not uniqueness, but superiority, or — put differently — which faith is right (and, of course, which ones must therefore be wrong).

My own thoughts on this are simple, but unsatisfactory to many; but I'll stick with them regardless of that. They are these. Jesus himself shows absolutely no interest and makes no assertions about either uniqueness or superiority. He assumes that his message of the kingdom of God is powerful and attractive, and he draws disciples to himself whom he teaches to observe his way of living in the world. By word and deed they are meant to witness to the truth of Jesus' words, life, cross, and resurrection, and reveal by their love and peacefulness a community oriented towards God. They are not meant to argue about God, but meant to show forth God. "Superiority" is simply not part of the message, and "uniqueness" is simply an indisputable fact. To the same extent that Christians have been true or false to Jesus' way, those of other beliefs (or no beliefs) will weigh its truth and value. The proof, as they say, is in the pudding. Christians who assert superiority might take note.

ALL THAT'S BEEN STATED so far has been my own understanding of the Christian mind and Christian freedom for as long as I can remember. I confess here at the outset that I believe, and always have, that the Christian faith has nothing to fear from dialogue with the other great faiths and philosophies of humankind. Marked differences and spiritual and human commonality exist simultaneously between religions. I choose to focus more on the commonality than on the differences, and leave the rest to God.

Huston Smith has suggested that human beings share, as it were, a common religious "grammar."[1] From the human person outward towards infinity we discover a shared vision of hierarchies and levels of reality; within the human person we find a common experience and a perception of depths capable of profound spiritual transformation. All the world's faiths reproduce this common grammar of spiritual experience and perception in one way or another.

As I said above, the classical Christian view (or at

1. Henry Rosemont Jr. and Huston Smith, *Is There a Universal Grammar of Religion?* (Peru, Ill.: Open Court Publishing Co., 2008).

least one significant version of it) has been to recognize the divine *logos* as shaping this common grammar in a hidden way, and revealing itself definitively in the person of Jesus Christ. Even if those of non-Christian faiths don't perceive that to be the case, we Christians neverthe-less can. If we think about it sufficiently long and hard enough (and assuming we have really encountered the pertinent texts and traditions firsthand and on their own terms, without prejudice or hubris), why shouldn't a Christian discern Christ and God, say, in the concept of the Tao, or in the words of Krishna to Arjuna in the Bhagavad Gita, or in the notion of the Buddha nature? This may even be one more way of understanding how Christ "is before all things, and in him all things hold to-gether" (Col. 1:17). Christians who seek to be followers of the way of Jesus should seek to "live peaceably with all" (Rom. 12:18), and perhaps the tacit recognition of Christ already at work in all faiths is a path towards achieving that. I'm certainly not the first to express such a view, but it bears repetition.

So, with these things in mind, I turn to the subject of this slim volume.

Back in 1982, I had the privilege of being asked to teach a religious studies course at the University of Mary-land, Baltimore County (UMBC). I was a young man at the time, just twenty-six, with nothing to show yet but a B.A. degree; so it was a great honor. It was to be a course on comparative contemplative traditions in the world's religions. Needless to say, it involved my becoming as thoroughly acquainted with my material as I could. I can't now recall if I was already aware of the Ten Ox-Herding Pictures in Zen Buddhism. It seems to me that I was. But, be that as it may, it was in the context of teaching that course that I began a reflection on them that has had a lasting influence on me. These images have remained fixed in my imagination as a sort of pictorial guide of the spiritual life. They have proved as applicable to my Christian spirituality as I know they have for countless Zen practitioners to theirs these past one thousand years.

I first saw them in that justly classic little book, *Zen Flesh, Zen Bones,* compiled by Paul Reps with the collaboration of Nyogen Senzaki,[2] a book I used with my students in that class at UMBC many years ago. Two other classic twentieth-century introductions to Zen Buddhism — D. T. Suzuki's *Manual of Zen Buddhism*[3] and Philip Kapleau's *The Three Pillars of Zen*[4] — were also helpful in my growing appreciation of the perennial usefulness of this unpretentious series of Zen icons. I still draw on these three books, and have done so for my own exploration here, although I depart from them all in various (peculiarly Christian) ways.

2. *Zen Flesh, Zen Bones: A Collection of Zen and Pre-Zen Writings,* compiled by Paul Reps and Nyogen Senzaki (New York: Doubleday-Anchor, 1961).

3. Daisetz Teitaro Suzuki, *Manual of Zen Buddhism* (New York: Grove Press, 1960).

4. Philip Kapleau, *The Three Pillars of Zen: Teaching, Practice, and Enlightenment* (New York: Anchor Books, 2000).

BEFORE TAKING another step towards a discussion of these pictures — their origin, purpose, and content — let me be clear that this is not a doctrinal or dogmatic book. Zen Buddhists may find fault with me in that I don't discuss at length the underlying principles of Buddhism, and perhaps they will justly wonder what a Christian is doing expounding on their iconography. All I can say in my defense is that I mean no disrespect; I want only to elucidate what I believe is there for all who seek enlightenment. That is, after all, what Zen imparts. And Zen is precisely the stripping down to the barest essentials for the sake of inner awakening. A Zen practitioner knows that if awakening occurs, all words and concepts are dispensable in the breakthrough of reality. What then of my words and concepts?

Some Christians may likewise wonder at the lack of interest I seem to have in clear, concise dogmatic and doctrinal formulations. I assure those readers that I am not ignorant of doctrinal matters and have spent years quite involved in them in very technical ways. But, at the end of the day, and at my age, I have come to value experience with God above discussion about God. In my youth I was a pugnacious defender of the faith. But now, having learned a few congenial things before my advancing dotage, I simply take God as a given. I take God as discernible but not definable, hidden and revealed, incomprehensible and everywhere present. He doesn't need my defense; he can take care of himself and advance his own cause. If there's one thing I've taken to heart from Martin Buber's *I and Thou*, it's this: God is al-

ways to be encountered directly, as *You* and not "it."[5]
Even when talking about God in objective "it" terms,
those terms are never final and always the beginning of
getting "it" wrong. When God is *You,* getting him wrong
is rarely a problem. This conviction has only increased in
me over the years, and the simplicity of this truth has al-
lowed me to view dogma as indicative rather than abso-
lute. What it indicates may be either a clear-cut path
through the woods to the dwelling of God, or a misleading way into a swamp of words and formulas and endless
definitions. Which one it will be all depends on how the
dogma is appropriated. God can never be reduced to re-
assuring abstractions (the principal sin of Job's friends),
can never be confined within a system of thought, and is
not the property of doctrines. God is *You* — the one "in
whom we live and move and have our being."

AND THAT BELIEF pretty well sets me straightway on the
path of those simple, beautiful, humble, humorous, and
joyful Ten Ox-Herding Pictures, which are nothing more
or less than a parable. I hope Buddhists will forgive a
Christian if he says he sees God in them.

5. Martin Buber, *I and Thou* (New York: Touchstone, 1996).

CHAPTER II

The Ten Ox-Herding Pictures: Their Origin

By the twelfth century A.D., Buddhism had already been in China for approximately one thousand years, and the Ch'an school of Buddhism had existed there since circa 500 A.D. It arrived, according to the tradition, with the legendary Bodhidharma (fl. 460-534), a Buddhist missionary monk from southern India. The word "ch'an" — the Chinese pronunciation of the Sanskrit word *dhyāna* — means "meditation," and it refers specifically to the type of sitting meditation in this particular stream of Mahayana Buddhism as taught by Bodhidharma. When this tradition took root in Japan in the twelfth century, "ch'an" became "zen," and we have come to know it best by its Japanese name.

In the same century that Ch'an Buddhism became Zen Buddhism in Japan, the Chinese Zen master Kakuan Shien (Kuo-an Shih-yuan) produced the pictures, poems, and commentaries we know as the Ten Ox-Herding Pictures. As far as I can tell, the poetry and commentaries that accompany each of the icons (and a preface to the set that I have never found in translation) are all that survive of Kakuan's oeuvre. Sadly, his original pictures are no longer extant. The versions which I have included in this volume are based on his originals.

The pictorial set of Kakuan is the one that was taken to Japan and became the standard one there. For Westerners, who got their knowledge of Zen through Japan, these pictures constitute the more familiar version as well. In China, another, earlier version of the pictures is more commonly known.

And that brings us to what we might plausibly suppose about Kakuan himself: that, although his set has undoubtedly become the most widely recognized and traditional form of the Ten Ox-Herding Pictures, it seems he was an innovator. Before he made his version, there were sets of five and six pictures with the motif of the Ox-Herder. But, before Kakuan, the concluding picture was that which now stands as the eighth in his arrangement. It is the picture of the empty circle (see Picture 8 below), which — as we shall see and say more about in its proper place — is the symbol of enlightenment. Kakuan, in contrast to those who preceded him in rendering the Ox-Herding motifs, didn't conclude with that image of transcendent bliss, as if enlightenment alone is enough for the practitioner of Zen. He went two steps beyond that with two new icons of his own invention: first, a beautiful evocation of the cycles of nature (the ninth picture), and then a world-affirming, crowning picture to conclude the set. The tenth picture depicts the enlightened one as a human being "with helping hands" mingling in society with other human beings.

For Kakuan it is evident that the Buddhist ideal of the *bodhisattva* — the enlightened one who works to bring "all sentient beings" (which means all "conscious" or sometimes all "living" beings) to spiritual awakening — is the greatest goal to which one can aspire in this life. Too often Westerners don't appreciate the paramount significance within Mahayana Buddhism of compassion for all sentient creatures. All the Zen schools stand within this tradition. We will return to this theme in due course; but it's worth noting here that the addition of these last two images, which don't leave us with the empty circle of transcendence as the series' final and apparently infinite goal, suggests as well that the search and the experience indicated in these Ten Pictures persist throughout one's life. One doesn't merely arrive once and for all at spiritual awakening, in other words, but instead must view its pursuit as an ongoing practical way of life. That these two observations (that the enlightened person returns to the world "with helping hands," and that meditative exercise is a way of life and not a one-time achievement) have parallels in the practice of Christian discipleship is a matter to which we will certainly return. So, as we can see, Kakuan innovatively added elements of profound significance to the motifs he inherited and reshaped.

Kakuan also provided pithy Zen poems to accompany each image. Not satisfied with the poetry alone, he added commentaries as well (or perhaps it was the other way around). In this he reminds me somewhat of John of the Cross, the great sixteenth-century Spanish Christian mystic. John wrote magnificent mystical poems about his experience of God. Urged on by those who sought to comprehend their meaning, he composed four books of commentary which have justly become major classics in the Christian contemplative tradition. At the heart of John's spirituality is what is known as *via negativa* ("negative path") mysticism. In the famous diagram of his mystical path, which he drew for his book *The Ascent of Mount Carmel*, John made such Zen-like assertions as these:

> To come to the knowledge of all, desire the knowledge of nothing.

> To come to enjoy what you have not, you must go by a way which you enjoy not.

> In this nakedness the spirit finds its quietude and rest, for in coveting nothing, nothing tires it by pulling it up, and nothing oppresses it by pushing it down, because it is in the center of its humility.

> Here there is no longer any way, because for the just man there is no law; he is a law unto himself.[1]

And so on.

With some obvious adjustment of language and concepts, these are ideas not entirely alien to the great themes

---

1. *The Collected Works of St. John of the Cross,* trans. Kieran Kavanaugh, O.C.D., and Otilio Rodriguez, O.C.D. (Washington, D.C.: ICS Publications, 1991), p. 111.

of Kakuan's Ten Pictures and the poems and commentaries he composed for them. As Abbot John Chapman noted in his *Spiritual Letters,* there is something "Buddhist" about John of the Cross;[2] and John C. H. Wu described his spirituality as "Taoistic."[3] And "Taoistic," of course, can just as aptly — indeed, considerably more so — describe the spiritual outlook of Kakuan. There is clearly as much Taoism as Buddhism in his Ten Ox-Herding Pictures, and one could in fact take them as purely Taoist.

Regarding Taoism, Lin Yutang summarized its fundamental beliefs this way: "It is a philosophy of the essential unity of the universe (monism), of reversion ["things revert to their original state; life is in constant flux and change"], polarization (*yin* and *yang*), and eternal cycles, of the leveling of all differences, the relativity of all standards, and the return of all to the Primeval One, the divine intelligence, the source of all things. From this naturally arises the absence of desire for strife and contention and fighting for advantage." Elsewhere, Lin Yutang had no qualms about referring to "the Primeval One" — the One from which the great *Tao* ("Way") comes — quite simply as "God." And, he continues, "Thus the teachings of humility and meekness of the

2. Abbot John Chapman, *Spiritual Letters* (London: Sheed & Ward, 1989), p. 269.

3. Quoted in Christopher Nugent, "Satori in St. John of the Cross," *Monastic Interreligious Dialogue Bulletin,* no. 47 (May 1993). Access this article at http://www.monasticdialog.com/a.php?id =356.

Christian Sermon on the Mount find a rational basis, and a peaceable temper is bred in man."[4]

D. T. Suzuki said of Zen that it was a movement in which "the Chinese mind completely asserted itself."[5] Influenced by both Confucianism and Taoism, Zen Buddhism developed a form and expression that was distinctively Chinese in character. One has only to look at the ninth of the Ox-Herding Pictures of Kakuan, "Returning to the Origin" or "Source," with its rendering of nature's twisting roots and flowering branches, and its hint of the Taoist concept of *Wu Wei* — "non-action" or "non-assertiveness" — in the midst of creation's movement and change, to hear the voices of Lao Tzu and Chuang Tzu singing through it.

The humor implicit in the images, too, resonates with Taoist *joie de vivre*. Taoist poets celebrate their wine, for example; and in the tenth ox-herding picture, lo and behold, the happy figure depicted there carries over his shoulder a wine gourd. Taoism rejoices in the harmony within nature and the goodness of it (even the earthy goodness of wine), and seeks to bring man back in line with his own true nature. It would bring us into cooperative flow with the source and never-ceasing origin of all things, with the Tao, or "Way," that governs

---

4. *The Wisdom of Lao Tzu*, translated, edited, and with an introduction and notes by Lin Yutang (New York: The Modern Library [Random House], 1948), p. 14.

5. Quoted in *A Source Book in Chinese Philosophy*, translated and compiled by Wing-Tsit Chan (Princeton: Princeton University Press, 1963), p. 425.

and moves creation effortlessly. Taoist meditation is intended to bring one realization of this formless, unitive, all-embracing, and ultimately nameless reality. Where Taoism speaks of the Tao, Zen Buddhism speaks of the Buddha-mind or Buddha-nature that is to be found in all things. The ox is a symbol common to both Taoism and Zen, and it refers in the latter to the primordial Buddha-nature or — what is the same thing — one's true nature or true mind. We will look at this more closely in the next chapter. (I shall only note here, with just a little hesitancy, that a Christian might well think of the Spirit of God as somewhat analogous to both the concept of the Tao — and its close linkage in Chinese thought with *te* — "power" or "virtue" — and the concept of the universally permeating Buddha-nature.)

Finally, the Ten Ox-Herding Pictures are typically Chinese in their pragmatic, this-worldly quality. In this they remind us of the plain and unsophisticated imagery of Jesus' parables. In many respects the Chinese mind resembles the Jewish mind. Wisdom is for practical application to real life as much in Chinese thought as in Jewish religion. There is a decided emphasis in both on the practical, the homely, the things of nature and human existence. Intricate theoretical systematizing, elaborate metaphysical argument, tortuous and labyrinthine logic — these were not indulged in by Chinese sages or Hebrew prophets and wise men as they were, say, among the contemporary representatives of the philosophies of Greece or the religions of India (including Buddhism).

As already mentioned, the eighth picture depicts symbolically the idea of transcendence and mystical attainment. It should also be noted that it depicts absolutely no heavenly vision or divine beings — just an empty circle. In its own way it is just as stern in its refusal to depict the holiest realities as the Hebrew tradition is. That which cannot be described or defined is left blank — undescribed and undefined. No attempts are made to provide a peek into celestial realms. After all . . .

> A way that can be walked
>   is not The Way.
> A name that can be named
>   is not The Name.

> Tao is both Named and Nameless.
> As Nameless, it is the origin of all things.
> As Named, it is the mother of all things.

> A mind free of thought,
>   merged within itself,
>   beholds the essence of Tao.
> A mind filled with thought,
>   identified with its own perceptions,
>   beholds the mere forms of this world . . .[6]

6. *Tao Te Ching: The Definitive Edition*, translation and commentary by Jonathan Star (New York: Jeremy P. Tarcher/Putnam, 2001), verse 1, p. 14.

These are, of course, the opening lines of the *Tao Te Ching*, or the book of *Lao Tzu*, written in the sixth century B.C., according to the traditional dating, although some scholars suggest that perhaps it was composed as late as the fourth and third centuries B.C. The insight expressed so unequivocally in these sentences is that no human concepts or ideas can ever express the experience of what entirely transcends human thought and imagination. It can be known directly, but not actually portrayed. The eighth of the Ox-Herding Pictures, and also the ninth in a completely different way, are perhaps the best illustrations of this ancient doctrine from the *Tao Te Ching*.

Surrounding this mere symbol of the circle are the other pictures in the set. They feature a boy, an ox, a wood, a hut, and a smiling, big-bellied sage. Nature is everywhere seen, quite this-worldly and down-to-earth. The story the pictures tell, like Jesus' parables, is simple and direct. A boy goes looking for an ox. He has to tame him, and he rides him back home. And then the story takes a whole new twist, and we discover that we're dealing with something much more profound and sublime. Suddenly the mystical experience is shown intersecting pragmatically with everyday life and in the process transfiguring it completely. But the mystical doesn't cancel out everyday life. There is a movement from transcendent awareness back to the dusty roads and to human life, as already mentioned.

Three of these symbols in the parable — very important ones — are what we will examine next.

CHAPTER III

The Ox, the Boy, and the Man

This is perhaps a good place to present brief introductions to three essential symbols in the Ten Pictures, although we will have more to say about each of them in the commentaries later. As already stated, the empty circle of the eighth picture is of crucial importance to the set. Before Kakuan's additions to the series, it was in fact the ultimate and crowning image. But three other prominent symbols are the Ox, the Boy, and the Man. A few words about them here will help us to look at these pictures with some key ideas already in mind.

So, we'll explore them one at a time.

First, *the Ox:* Paul Reps refers to the Ox in *Zen Flesh, Zen Bones* as the "Bull," but I have no idea whether or not the original designation entailed any distinction between "ox" and "bull." I rather doubt it. The more common word used in translation is "ox," and so I've gone along with the majority and stuck with that term.

But, whether bull or ox, bovines have been important in many, if not most, periods and cultures around the globe. From prehistoric cave paintings to primitive rituals of slaughter, from the choreographed cruelty of the Spanish bull-ring to the veneration accorded it in India, from Audumbla in Norse myth to the red heifer of Hebrew sacrifice to the bison of the American plains, the bull has been a staple of life and service, and consequently a potent symbol. Sacred, profane, wild, domesticated, grazer, source of sustenance, beast of burden and plower of fields; at once the embodiment of awesome beauty, natural grace, and brute power — all this can be declared of cattle as employed by man for his various ends throughout the ages. In Taoism the bull is a symbol of life; in Buddhism, with its Indian origin, it is revered.

When we turn to our simple Ten Pictures, what is the Ox? Is it sacred or natural or profane? In typical Zen fashion, the answer is "Yes." One of the goals of these pictures is to show us how meaningless such distinctions as "sacred," "natural," and "profane" really are. Reps says that the Ox "is the eternal principle of life, truth in action."[1] Philip Kapleau writes, "It is probably because of the sacred nature of the ox in ancient India that this animal came to be used to symbolize Primordial Nature or Buddha-mind."[2] All this is true, but it may need some

1. *Zen Flesh, Zen Bones: A Collection of Zen and Pre-Zen Writings*, compiled by Paul Reps and Nyogen Senzaki (New York: Doubleday-Anchor, 1961), p. 134.

2. Philip Kapleau, *The Three Pillars of Zen: Teaching, Practice, and Enlightenment* (New York: Anchor Books, 2000), p. 332.

fine-tuning to suggest what this might mean for us and our own spiritual lives.

One of the first things we will be told about the Ox in the Ten Pictures is that, although the Boy goes in search of him, he was never really lost in the first place. We are meant to perceive that the Ox and the Boy are in some way actually one, that the division between them is an illusion that must be overcome. Throughout the sequence of pictures we must keep in mind that the series is about meditation and the effect that meditation is supposed to accomplish in us.

In point of fact, the Boy is searching for the Ox within himself, and the Ox is his true self. (I use the slippery word "self" in a non-technical way, meaning by it the essential spirit underlying an individual's identity and outward personas.) Through distractions — arising in us because of the bustling world, because of unruly senses and mental wanderings — one loses sight of what one truly is. The Ox — the true self — needs to be tracked, tamed, and ridden home. In other words, the practitioner of Zen meditation must find out what and who he is, where his contentment lies, and his own abiding but unknown rootedness in the Origin and Source of all things.

The Ox is therefore sacred and natural and profane all at once, because he embraces all of life. As Buddha-mind or Buddha-nature (or the Tao), he really is everywhere and never lost; but in each one of us, as the principle of our being and consciousness, he must be sought. If there is something like a primordial "fall" in this story, it is a "fall" from the original grace of experiencing our union with the transcendent principle that indwells our deepest selves. If we don't look for that true nature in our selves, we'll never know it, and we'll remain lost, alienated, and disconnected. We may as a substitute for such experience — the real meaning of our existence — fill our minds with cheap thrills and accumulated stuff instead, keeping ourselves distracted and as artificially stimulated as we can. If we don't look for the Ox, we will just wander through life, lost and preoccupied with greed and fear and useless amusements. And then we'll die — and very possibly we'll die discontented, anxious, confused, and desperate.

Finding the Ox, mastering him, knowing him, accepting him — that's the goal set before us in these Ten Pictures. The Ox is both within us and outside us — the life and nature in us is the same that flows through all creation. We are essentially one with the principle of all things, no matter how obscured that ceaseless union has become to our minds. To discover the truth in our selves is to find unity and peace and satisfaction.

In the next chapter we will look at ways a Christian can interpret this in the language of his or her own tradition. But for now it's enough to say that the Ox symbolizes what we are as substantially part of God's universe. The beginning of grace, to use Christian terms, is to return to our true nature and true mind in Christ, and to escape from the futility of an ersatz self formed in an artificial and impermanent environment. (It is also worth remarking that in other versions of the Ten Ox-Herding Pictures, the Ox is first dark in hue and gradually becomes lighter. Eventually he disappears from view alto-gether, as he does also in Kakuan's pictures. The implica-tion of these other versions, however, is that there has been an accumulation of dirt and grime that has ob-scured the Ox's natural whiteness, and that over time — through the practice of meditation — this layer of ob-scuring muck is cleansed away.)

WE TURN our attention now to *the Boy*.

He is young, and therefore he is a *learner*. Another word for "learner" is "disciple," and the Boy (never mind the sex — the point isn't the sex, but the youthfulness of the main character) is the quintessential image of the dis-ciple. No matter what the age of the pupil might be, eight or eighty, he is youthful and childlike. As in the Christian Gospels, where Jesus uses the model of the child to em-phasize the need for teachableness and openness, here the disciple is also childlike.

Disciple though the Boy is, however, the Ten Pictures show no teacher for him. Is he then on his own as he seeks for the Ox? In a way, yes. Every disciple and practi-tioner of meditation is alone within himself or herself. Even if the disciple is surrounded by other disciples, the inner search and effort is something that is undertaken individually. The paradox, of course, is that the goal is to find that principle which unites us with everything har-moniously. But the search within for our true nature is a solitary endeavor.

Nevertheless, one can be certain that, as a Zen practi-tioner, the "Boy" — the disciple — has a master. This master, however, stands outside the purview of the pictures themselves, which illustrate the inner dimension of the seeking disciple's mind. The master — standing behind the pictures, so to speak, and hidden from view — is the one who provides the pictures in the first place. The master of the Ten Pictures still teaches, then, and we even know his name. It's Zen Master Kakuan, and he continues teaching his disciples just as Jesus still teaches us when we listen to his parables. The master isn't in the pictures, and Jesus isn't in the parables; but still these great teachers guide us invisibly through them.

The Boy is not just young, but a *searcher*. As such he works hard. He's not lazy; he's serious about the search for the Ox. Disciples, likewise, are meant to work and to practice, and not become lazy. Meditation — especially in the Zen tradition — involves effort, both mental and physical. Nothing can be achieved in meditation, any more than in any other serious pursuit, without exertion and dedication. But, as we shall see, effort and dedication lead to effortlessness, bliss, and peace — a spiritually natural "going with the flow."

LASTLY, WHO IS *the Man* in the tenth picture?

When I was a boy, my parents had a small wooden figure of Hotei in the house. He was big-bellied, grinning (with little white inlaid teeth), bare-chested, and carrying a large sack in Santa Claus fashion. My brother and I were informed that he was "the Chinese god of luck," and that rubbing his belly would bring good fortune. Luck-bestowing or not, the statuette was a particular favorite of mine, and there was something so jolly about Hotei that just seeing his stout form was enough to bring cheer. To this day he remains a much-loved image for me.

The name "Hotei" is actually the Japanese version of the Chinese "Budai," and it means "Cloth Sack." Perhaps the name "Budai" — and the fact that historically he was a Ch'an Buddhist monk of the tenth century — has contributed to his being mistakenly identified with Shakyamuni "Buddha." He is often called "the laughing Buddha," which is fair enough. His head is shaved in Buddhist monastic style, and he is usually portrayed carrying or wearing his prayer beads. He is the bringer of joy and contentment. Happiness is his chief characteristic. Taoist folk tradition has numbered him among the Seven Lucky Gods; and he is a "patron saint," so to speak, of a number of professional groups, including (rather understandably) bartenders and (not so understandably) politicians. He is also a patron of children, a sort of Chinese St. Nicholas, and often shown with children around him. According to legend, the sack he carries contains sweets for children, and food and drink for the poor.

As mentioned, he was by all accounts a good-natured Zen Buddhist monk, living two centuries before Kakuan produced his version of the Ten Ox-Herding Pictures. Hotei achieved enlightenment, and subsequently was regarded as an incarnation of the bodhisattva, Maitreya. A *bodhisattva*, you may recall, is a *buddha* ("awakened one") whose chief aim, born of universal compassion, is to bring others to enlightenment. Hotei is, therefore, a bodhisattva himself, an incarnation of great compassion and infinite generosity.

One story survives about Hotei, or Budai, in his capacity as a Zen master, which may be telling for us. As Hotei was journeying one day, another monk asked him, "What is the meaning of Zen?" Hotei simply dropped his sack to the ground. The monk persisted: "How does one realize Zen?" Hotei picked up his sack again and continued along the path.

A strange story, certainly, and not one that needs lengthy explanation — in Zen, actions speak for themselves. But it is the second action, that of Hotei walking on down the path, that may speak directly to Kakuan's novel inclusion of him in his final picture of the ox-herding series (for it is certainly the image of Hotei that he draws on for that icon). My suggestion is this: In the story, Hotei, by walking on, invites the other monk to follow him and observe his method of realizing Zen (as Jesus calls his disciples to "come and see" and follow him). By putting Hotei in his final picture, Kakuan is similarly offering this compassionate, generous bodhisattva as a model of what a life committed to the spiritual path of enlightenment should ultimately look like. That it isn't an ascetic, somber, serious image is important. Instead, we have a bliss-bestowing, smiling, world-affirming, happy-go-lucky saint who — in addition to his massive sack of gifts and his walking staff — is carrying a gourd of wine.

WHAT WE SHALL SEE as we look at Kakuan's pictures in sequence, and read his poems and commentaries, is that the Ox, the Boy, and the Man are one and the same. The Boy, the disciple, searches for himself — his true nature, his "Buddha-nature" — which is represented by the image of the Ox. Finally, enlightened and whole, he returns to the world as a man — and not just a man, but a bodhisattva like Hotei, whose joviality and ample charity bring even withered trees to life again.

Kakuan's point is quite straightforward with his addition of the last two pictures. Buddhahood or enlightenment isn't simply what occurs during meditation; otherwise, one would cease to have "Buddha-nature" or a "true nature" as soon as one stopped meditating. If that were the case, of course, one would be right to end the Ox-Herding Pictures at the eighth picture, and allow the empty circle to remain the final, conclusive image of transcendence achieved. By making the tenth picture the concluding one, Kakuan shows that Buddhahood resides in the one who has returned to the world to mingle with the people with generosity, joyfulness, humility, and naturalness (no sign of being holier-than-thou or demonstratively pious). Grace is seen not in outward displays of religiosity, ascetic sensationalism, or miracles, but in the natural ease of one who has found his true self and can dwell without defense against or offense towards others. Such a one effortlessly radiates a life-giving presence.

Taken together, then, the Ten Ox-Herding Pictures as presented in Kakuan's version teach that the path of our own enlightenment should awaken in us a great aptitude for love.

CHAPTER IV

The Ox-Herder and the Good Shepherd

As the last few paragraphs above should suggest, there exists between the spiritual outlook of the Ten Ox-Herding Pictures and the teachings of Christ a similar ideal. Put most simply, it's this: *Authentic* spiritual life must begin with an inner transformation of one's self, and must lead to an outward life that is natural and loving.

In contrast, of course, there is an *inauthentic* spiritual life, one which is a matter of external practices and customs, which engages in outward show and pretended pieties, and involves neither serious inner discipline (such as meditation) nor an increase of sympathy towards others.

Both Buddha and Christ taught that true religion was a matter of the depths, of interior transformation, and that it must result in compassion. Buddha called it "awakening," and Jesus called it "the kingdom of God" — but both meant a profound revolution within oneself that led to the reordered and correct perception of all things. The differences between Jesus and Buddha are evident on the surface. The commonality is evident, too, if one takes the time to read, say, the Sermon on the Mount and the *Dhammapada* back-to-back.[1] On a deeper level, that of the practice of meditation or contemplative prayer and its consequences in practitioners' behavior, the commonality becomes even more pronounced. The question soon ceases to be "Which one of these visions is true?" and instead becomes "How is it that two very different traditions possess so much truth in common?" Only the most anti-religious bigot would hesitate to call what they have in common "truth."

The image of "searching" is, of course, one we see in the Gospels. Jesus, using the model of the shepherd, depicts his search for the lost and wandering sheep — that is, the human person (see, for example, Matt. 18:10-14; Luke 15:1-7; John 10:11-18; Luke 19:10). The similarity with the Boy searching for the Ox in Kakuan's ox-herding pictures appears superficial if we compare it to Jesus' image of the shepherd looking for the lost sheep. After all, the Boy's search for the Ox, as we said above, is an internal quest — something not actually done externally but in the depths of one's spirit. He searches subjectively for himself. Jesus' image suggests, instead, God "outside," objectively searching for us.

That is, as I said, the superficial observation. One

---

1. See my book *Taking Jesus at His Word: What Jesus Really Said in the Sermon on the Mount* (Grand Rapids: Wm. B. Eerdmans, 2012).

might suggest, however, that the way the shepherd searches for and brings back the lost sheep (and likewise, in the other parables of Luke 11, how the woman lights a lamp to seek for her lost coin, and how the prodigal son comes to his senses and returns to his father's house) is through an inner work directly on and through a person's heart and mind: God seeking us within our own subjective searching. We call this the work of God's Holy Spirit (or "Holy Breath") in Christianity, awakening us to our distance from God and the need to search for him. It is within us that the Shepherd seeks us, working through us and guiding us towards himself.

Still, a closer analogy is the image of searching for (and finding) the kingdom of God in other parables of Jesus. Perhaps the most familiar is this: "Again, the kingdom of heaven is like a merchant in search of fine pearls, who, on finding one pearl of great value, went and sold all that he had and bought it" (Matt. 13:45-46). As I have written in three previous books,[2] the kingdom of God is both an outer, communal reality and an inner, transformative presence in the teachings of Christ. One of the apocryphal sayings found in *The Gospel of Thomas* (logion 3) puts it succinctly, and reflects accurately what is indicated throughout the New Testament regarding this vital concept: "The kingdom is inside of you and outside of

---

2. See *Taking Jesus at His Word;* and also *Knowing Darkness: On Skepticism, Melancholy, Friendship, and God* (Grand Rapids: Wm. B. Eerdmans, 2009); and *The Yoke of Jesus: A School for the Soul in Solitude* (Grand Rapids: Wm. B. Eerdmans, 2010).

you." The better-known version of this saying is that of Luke 17:20-21: "The kingdom of God is not coming with signs to be observed; nor will they say, 'Lo, here it is!' or 'There!' for behold, the kingdom of God is in the midst of you." If one is looking for the kingdom of God, then, one begins within. Indeed, it begins as a "seed" planted deep within the one who assimilates Jesus' message (see Matt. 13:1-9 and parallels, Mark 4:1-9 and Luke 8:4-8). That it is an interior transformation of the person is underscored by the apostle Paul's description of the kingdom as "righteousness and peace and joy in the Holy Spirit" (Rom. 14:17).

The growth of the kingdom is also depicted in terms of nature. Taoism and Zen Buddhism also highlight the naturalness of both spiritual enlightenment and the character of the awakened person. The enlightened one is not a "supernatural" person, nor even one who appears to be "preternatural" — rather, he is wholly "natural," because he has found genuine inner harmony with the Origin and Source of all nature (see picture 9 below). Jesus' description of the inner and outer development of the kingdom is reminiscent of this: "The kingdom of God is as if a man should scatter seed upon the ground, and should sleep and rise night and day, and the seed should sprout and grow, he knows not how. The earth produces of itself, first the blade, then the ear, then the full grain in the ear. But when the grain is ripe, at once he puts in the sickle, because the harvest has come" (Mark 4:26-29). Action and effort attend the beginning and end result of the growth, but there is "effortless action" at work in the interior growth of the kingdom of God. It not only resembles how nature "produces of itself," but also shows how natural God's kingdom essentially is — the God of the kingdom within is also the God of nature without. Both quite naturally (!) work in the same effortlessly productive way. Both are living. There is not only resemblance between the two, but an original identity.

Lastly, as we saw with Kakuan's crowning of his set of images with the vivacious figure of Hotei, the goal of "Buddha-mind" is to shine with generosity and love among the people of the world. There is little need to cite the multitude of passages in the New Testament which make it clear that Jesus' goal for his disciples is also a luminous practice of love towards even the most unlovely. Just as Kakuan could not leave his followers with the misleading impression that private transcendence (picture 8) is the last word in the purpose of Zen practice, neither could Paul leave his readers with any mistaken notion of what the crowning purpose of Jesus' message means in practice: "And if I have prophetic powers, and understand all mysteries and all knowledge, and if I have all faith, so as to remove mountains, but have not love, I am nothing. . . . So faith, hope, love abide, these three; but the greatest of these is love" (1 Cor. 13:2, 13).

So, as in Buddhism, solitary contemplative practice is encouraged for Jesus' disciples: "But when you pray, go into your room and shut the door and pray to your Father who is in secret" (Matt. 6:6). But, as also in Buddhism, the goal is love, both love for the transcendent (see picture 8 below) and love — compassion — for human beings (see picture 10 below): "You shall love the Lord your God with all your heart, and with all your soul, and with all your mind. This is the great and first commandment. And a second is like it: You shall love your neighbor as yourself. On these two commandments depend all the law and the prophets" (Matt. 22:37-40).

Or, as the teachings of the Buddha preserved in the *Dhammapada* phrase it right in the very first chapter, "Hate is not conquered by hate: hate is conquered by love. This is a law eternal. . . . Those who know the Real is, and know the unreal is not, they shall indeed reach the Truth, safe on the path of right thought."[3]

---

3. *The Dhammapada*, translated from the Pali and with an introduction by Juan Mascaró (London: Penguin Books, 1973), 1:5, 12, pp. 35-36.

CHAPTER V

Exploring the Ox-Herding Pictures

About the Pictures and Text

The version of the Ten Ox-Herding Pictures that I've provided below is that of the fifteenth-century Japanese Zen monk Shubun. The original is rendered on a paper handscroll in ink and light shades of bronze, brown, and beige. (The scroll's dimensions are 32 centimeters in height by 181.5 centimeters in length, and each picture has a diameter of 14 centimeters.) The scroll is housed in the museum of the Shôkoku-ji Temple in Kyoto. I've never seen the original, although I hope I may have that opportunity one day; but it is my favorite version of the series, and I would have chosen it for this book even if it hadn't been "in the public domain" already. It is said that Shubun copied it directly from Kakuan's original series.

Kakuan accompanied each of these visual "koans" with a poem of his own composition, and a commentary for each poem and picture as well. The versions below of the poems and commentaries are my own reworking, based on the translations found in Reps, Suzuki, and Kapleau.[1] I have, whether technically right or wrong, retained Reps's first-person singular throughout instead of Suzuki's and Kapleau's use of "he" and "him." One obvious concern was to be as gender-inclusive as possible. But perhaps even of greater significance to me was the desire to make these renditions as *personal* as possible. Third-person language distances the reader. First-person language brings the reader into the text much more directly. Since these texts deal with the observer's inner life, with his or her "search for the Ox," and since every disciple who turns to these pictures and texts for inspiration is interiorly the Ox-Herder, the use of "I" seemed to me to be fitting.

Lastly, each poem and commentary is followed by my own explicitly Christian comments on the Ten Pictures. Just as I would welcome a Buddhist reflection on, say, the Way of the Cross, so I trust that a Christian reflection on these brilliant Zen Buddhist icons will be welcome. The theme of the series is universal and applicable to any one of the great religious traditions. It tells a perennial truth about the inner work of discipleship, and reminds us all that contemplation without loving action is incomplete.

1. See *Zen Flesh, Zen Bones: A Collection of Zen and Pre-Zen Writings,* compiled by Paul Reps and Nyogen Senzaki (New York: Doubleday-Anchor, 1961); Daisetz Teitaro Suzuki, *Manual of Zen Buddhism* (New York: Grove Press, 1960); Philip Kapleau, *The Three Pillars of Zen: Teaching, Practice, and Enlightenment* (New York: Anchor Books, 2000).

Indeed, contemplation and meditation exist to deepen our empathy with all persons and all things. It isn't a solitary endeavor only, and "enlightenment" and "the kingdom of God" are put to the test and manifested by an increase in active compassion.

That was Kakuan's message, as it was Buddha's before him. And it is unquestionably the supreme business of the disciples of Jesus Christ as well.

1. Seeking the Ox

Alone in the wilderness, lost in the jungles,
    I look for the Ox,
Which I do not find.
Following unnamed swelling rivers, treading
    interpenetrating paths on faraway mountains,
My strength failing, near despair, I carry on
    my search for the Ox I cannot find.
At night I hear only cicadas singing in the
    maple-woods.

The Ox has never really gone astray, so why am I searching for it? Because I turned my back on my own true nature, I cannot find him. My senses have become deluded, confused, and I can't even see his tracks. My home is receding further and further away from me; and suddenly I'm confronted by many crisscrossing paths! Which one I should take I can't tell. Greed for worldly gain and fear of loss spring up like fire. Ideas of right and wrong come at me like daggers.

There are a number of ways a modern person can look at the Ten Ox-Herding Pictures. One particularly fruitful approach could be a Jungian one. The Boy in such an interpretation might represent the conscious mind and the Ox the subconscious within a single person. The Boy looks for and brings the Ox out into the light, just as the conscious mind opens itself to the mysterious and elusive subconscious and learns to cooperate with it. The two come together, learn to work in harmony, and, united, they grow into full maturity. This might prove a genuinely perceptive way of viewing the series, and it wouldn't be very far from the original theme. The series is about maturity, and maturity — as Jung himself well knew — involves a spiritual life of depth.

A person's conscious self must come to terms with its immature, unstable qualities so long as it exists on the superficial level of the ego, which is the "mask" one has shaped in life to exist in society. At some point in life, one may suddenly realize that this superficial, artificial persona can't be maintained, that something deeply suppressed longs to get out, and a crisis is imminent if something doesn't change. Such moments upset a person's ideas of the status quo, and such a crisis can in fact be dangerous. People frequently do foolish things in such instances. But it is also true that people can make right decisions in the face of revelations of the fragility and illusory nature of their identity.

The state of mind described in the first of the Ten Pictures is similar to the sort of personal crisis I've touched on above. Confusion, disorientation, loneliness, fear, and a sense of loss; the idea that "home" (not something to be identified simply in geographical terms) has been left far behind and one cannot find one's way back — these are common feelings of anxiety, stress, and *angst*. They are not confined to any single stage of life. The Boy represents immaturity, but also discipleship.

Disciples are, almost by definition, "young," regardless of the actual years they have lived. Youth, the middle-aged, and the elderly can all have a deep awareness of having lost the way. For example, Dante begins his *Divine Comedy* by describing how, in the midst of his life (when he is about thirty-five years old), he has lost his way in a dark wood and is stalked by predators that symbolize his own disturbed passions. As he progresses with his guides — Virgil, St. Bernard, and Beatrice — from hell, through purgatory, and into heaven, he is in the position of questioner and (occasionally scared) follower. He is, in some sense, both the great poet and (in terms of our pictures) the lost Boy.

The Boy who seeks the Ox is aware that he has "turned his back" on his "true nature," and that he is, in a way, faced with "greed for worldly gain and fear of loss," and he is troubled by "ideas of right and wrong." The initial surprise of the Ten Pictures is the revelation that *he* is the one who has gone astray, *not the Ox.* We are told right at the outset that the Ox has in fact never wandered off. He is right where he belongs, doing whatever an Ox does, in accord with his nature. Our subconscious might be described as doing precisely the same. The Zen Buddhist would say that the Ox is the Buddha-nature, and that it is there all the time within us, waiting to be found — just as it is present and infinitely patient within everyone and everything. A Taoist might see in it the Tao we should be following, perhaps even identifying it imaginatively with the water buffalo that the great sage Lao Tzu, according to legend, rode upon as he disappeared into the west. At any rate, it's the Boy, not the Ox, who is lost, scared, troubled, and off-course. And now life has suddenly presented him with numerous crisscrossing paths — utter confusion! And the question is simple but hard: Which way to follow?

The choices he faces are astutely reduced to greed and fear, right and wrong. The way of greed — the accumulation of things, the endless consumption of stuff that is pitched to us as "necessary," but that is merely exploiting our tendencies to self-indulgence ("because," we're told, we "deserve it") — appears now to the Boy to be unsatisfying and distracting. The fear of losing what one has "in the bank," so to speak — goods, looks, youth, wealth, health, life itself — is distracting in a very different but related way, filling the Boy with anxiety at every remembrance that everything and everyone is impermanent. And then, nagging and gnawing at the fabricated self with its concerns for self-survival and maintenance of the status quo, there are the mental complexities of trying to untangle right from wrong as the need for change threatens and beckons. What is the right way, and how should we walk in it?

As I have already suggested, if there is a "fall" narrative in these Ten Pictures, it's to be found here. There is no story of a primordial loss of Eden, of course; but, if we're able to see it, this first picture is a suggestion of the loss each of us has sustained. It's the evocation of an existential revelation, something like the prodigal son's "coming to his senses" in Jesus' parable (Luke 15:17). The Boy, like the prodigal, is all at once shocked to find that his life is in a mess. He starts out to find the Ox, but he discovers that he has lost his way — in fact, he lost it long before he even set out on the search. He lost it when he turned his back on his true nature. Similarly, what the prodigal son wants is the way back "home," back to his father (the origin), and, in the language of Jesus, the kingdom of God. In Christian terms, the kingdom of God is always there within us, just as it is everywhere, and if we find it, we have found harmony with God and nature. It repairs the catastrophe of the "fall."

The ancient Chinese sage Mencius (fourth century B.C.) speaks along similar lines about what each man and woman has lost. In his famous parable about the deforestation of Ox Mountain (again, the Ox), which describes a kind of "fall" scenario, he says, "There was a time when the trees were luxuriant on Ox Mountain." But, he tells us, people have so denuded the mountain of its trees in order to build a metropolis that the mountain is now quite bald and without any vestige of its old beauty. "People, seeing only its baldness, tend to think that it never had any trees," he continues. Mencius then asks the incisive questions that lead up to his chief point: "But can this possibly be the nature of a mountain?" and "Can what is in man be completely lacking in decency and kindness? One's letting go of his true heart is like the case of the tree and the axes." Mencius goes on to say that if men continue to hack down every new sprout of a tree trying to grow again on Ox Mountain, eventually the normally regenerative powers of air and night will lack the ability to restore the mountain's original beauty. In like

44

manner, human beings can so ruin their true nature, with its original inclinations to goodness, that it will eventually wither away. (In his book Mencius touchingly refers to this original nature of humanity as "the lost child's heart.") Mencius concludes his parable by citing his master: "Confucius said, 'Hold on to it and it will remain; let go of it and it will disappear. One never knows the time it comes or goes, neither does one know the direction.' It is perhaps to the heart this refers."[2]

The Boy in the Ten Pictures has not held on to his "heart" — his heart is in fact "the Ox" which he seeks. It's not the physical heart that Mencius means, but something closer to that level within that goes under various names — the spirit, the Buddha-nature, the true self, the hidden Tao, the subconscious mind. It is, in the terms Jesus used, that place in us where the regenerative seeds of the kingdom are planted and take root. The Boy's loss, then, is the "fall" which every human person knows. Something that is essential to us is perceived as present, and yet we're lacking it. Something "original," something from our Origin, something we should have if we were at "home" with the Father — inner stability, harmony, peace, kindness, goodness (which should come naturally to us), and more. We don't know how to hold on to it, as Confucius suggested. "Can what is in man be completely lacking in decency and kindness?" asks Mencius. His an-

2. *Mencius,* VI, A, 8. I haven't followed a single translation here, but I have depended for the most part on *Mencius,* translated and with an introduction by D. C. Lau (London: Penguin Books, 1970).

swer is that it shouldn't be lacking, although we feel that it is; and we must recover it if we've lost touch with it.

Turning to another Chinese classic, the *Tao Te Ching*, which also provides concepts that underlie the Ten Pictures and which shares the concern of Mencius for recovering what we most need in human life, we hear that it isn't a set of rules or a body of laws that we are after. The Ox that the Boy seeks is not "goodness" in the restricted sense of mere morality or law. Moralism, especially on the superficial ego level of our existence, is part of the problem. This is why the Boy can say (much to our surprise, perhaps) that "ideas of right and wrong come at [him] like daggers." The Tao (the "Way") or, in Zen terms, the universal "Buddha-nature/mind" is a natural, flowing conformity with all that is naturally good. So, for that matter, is the kingdom of God, in which right and wrong are meant to flow through one's actions as naturally as the wind blows where it will (see John 3:8). However, as soon as one begins introducing formal laws, abstract concepts of right and wrong, one is mired in the complexities of categories and definitions, of opposites and ideas. The answer to the problem comes from the sage Lao Tzu, who is speaking here to those who guide others:

Abandon [mere concepts of] holiness
Discard cleverness
   and the people will benefit a hundredfold
Abandon the rules of [what is superficially
categorized as] "kindness"

46

Discard [what are defined abstractly as]
    "righteous" actions
  and the people will return
  to their own natural affections . . .

These lessons are mere elaborations
The essence of my teachings is this:
    See with original purity
    Embrace with original simplicity
    Reduce what you have
    Decrease what you want . . .[3]

Again, this is the Ox being sought by the Boy; the Ox has no consciousness of greed and fear, and lives free of complex but shallow "ideas of right and wrong." He is the enigmatic, semi-hidden embodiment of "original purity" and "original simplicity."

Here we can turn to the Christian vision and, in particular, to the insights of St. Paul with fresh understanding. The human race and each member of it is off-course, in a situation of "sin." Unfortunately, "sin" is a term that has become too much weighted with conceptual baggage for us. We hear it and assume more than the word is meant to convey. The word is not synonymous with sheer wickedness or vileness. It describes an unfortunate condition, not a malicious infraction. The word most fre-

3. *Tao Te Ching: The Definitive Edition*, translation and commentary by Jonathan Star (New York: Jeremy P. Tarcher/Putnam, 2001), verse 19, p. 23.

quently translated as "sin" in the New Testament is the Greek word *hamartia*. It was a term used often, for example, by Aristotle, among others. Literally it means "going wrong" or "going off-course." It has the same meaning as the confused condition of the Boy in the Ten Pictures — a state of having gone astray and gotten lost, and not necessarily being "evil" or naturally "depraved."

So it is that Paul writes, "All have sinned [*hemarton:* "gone astray"] and fall short of the glory of God" (Rom. 3:23). "Original purity" and "original simplicity," in other words, have been lost. Paul, in the same letter, describes painstakingly how even a mind predisposed to doing good nonetheless finds itself incapable of guiding one's life rightly: "I do not understand my own actions. For I do not do what I want, but I do the very thing I hate. . . . [It is] sin [*hamartia*] which dwells within me" (Rom. 7:15, 20).

He continues, "I see in my members another law at war with the law of my mind . . . the law of sin [*hamartia*]" (Rom. 7:23). Think of "law" here as if it was the "law" of gravity — something pulls us off-course, away from our own true nature. We have turned our backs on it. Each person's predicament is that he or she has lost God by losing his or her true nature and original purity.

Paul, like Lao Tzu, sees no help coming from the direction of laws, rules, complex definitions, and moral categorizations. Rather, it is through the "grace" of Christ that one is brought back to the way of God and to one's true nature.

That "grace" (which means "gift") begins, as in this

48

first of the Ten Pictures, with the crucial awareness of our condition of being lost, of being in a state of *ha-martia*. Once we see the tangled jungle and multiple paths as the confused mental mess they are, and look without illusions at our interior muddle and fears, we may also discover that, if we seek for it, what we most need has never in fact left us ("the kingdom of God is within you"). *We* have left *it* — or at least direct interaction with it; yet it remains, abiding inside us and doing whatever it does, patient and just being itself, like the Ox. Without coming to our senses like the prodigal son or the Boy in the Ten Pictures, we won't know to look for what can bring us home.

Paradoxically, what will carry us there is the waiting Ox.

2. Finding Footprints

Along the riverbank and under the trees
I find scattered footprints.
The sweet-scented grasses grow thick —
*   have I found the way?*
No matter how deep the gorges of these
*   faraway mountains,*
The Ox's nose cannot be hidden —
It reaches right up to heaven!

Through the sutras and the teachings I have come to under-
stand something; I have found the footprints of the Ox. I now
know that, just as many different-shaped gold vessels are all
made of one and the same gold, so each and every thing is a
reflection of the Self. But I still cannot distinguish what is
good from what is not; my mind is still confused about truth
and untruth. I haven't yet entered the gate, but tentatively I
have seen the footprints.

The commentary of Kakuan tells us exactly what he means by the metaphor of the Ox's footprints: the indications of that which he seeks in "the sutras and the teachings" — in other words, in his scriptures and tradition.

The sutras are the Buddhist scriptures, containing the alleged dialogues and sermons of the Buddha. The primary goal in Zen is direct experience of enlightenment through meditation, something which cannot be imparted merely through words or doctrines. Nevertheless, the Buddhist scriptures are of great importance to Zen practitioners. When the Boy, the disciple, in the poem and commentary says that he has found the Ox's footprints amid the moral confusion and mental desperation he has faced (the "jungle"), he means that he has seen the traces that lead towards the transcendent reality he seeks. Something in the scriptures and the teachings he has heard has stirred in him the hope that his search won't be in vain. "I haven't yet entered the gate," he confesses, "but tentatively I have seen the footprints."

But in the poem we hear that he has also seen more than just traces of the Ox. The Ox is apparently an immense creature, one who stands between heaven and earth: "No matter how deep the gorges of these faraway mountains,/ The Ox's nose cannot be hidden — /It reaches right up to heaven!"

This image is both comical and suggestive. It's *comical* in the sense that we can expect, quite rightly, a happy ending for the Boy's pursuit. And it's *suggestive* in the sense that the Ox represents, in paradoxical fashion, something that is simultaneously hidden and yet vast and impossible to conceal. The Ox's nose — certainly not the largest portion of the animal — is discernible above mountain peaks and reaches to heaven itself.[4]

4. I should mention that Reps has a different translation, and I think a far less interesting one: "Those traces can no more be hidden than one's nose, looking heavenward." Both Suzuki and Kapleau have

This same paradox is stated in the commentary in quite different terms: "I now know that, just as many different-shaped gold vessels are all made of one and the same gold, so each and every thing is a reflection of the Self." The key point of this enigmatic statement is this: all things, even if immeasurably diverse and dissimilar to each another, share in a commonality of being. All possess, in Buddhist terminology, the Buddha-nature. Everything participates in essential unity, whether conscious of the fact or not. And we are all made of the same "stuff" — we are all vessels made of the same gold — and we are all reflections of the same hidden and self-revealing Self.

If that is off-putting at first to some Christian sensibilities, it might help to recall that God is the one "in whom we live and move and have our being" (Acts 17:28), and that the ultimate realization of God is that we should see him "all in all" (1 Cor. 15:28, KJV).

The idea behind both images — the Ox, whose heaven-touching nose cannot be hid, and that of the myriad things made of one substance — is simply this: the great mystery sought by the disciple is at once both hidden and manifested. It is "the Self" working within all things which is also, in fact, present within him and impelling him to search for it.

What guides him on now, though not without some hesitancy and questioning on his part, are the footprints of the Ox — that is to say, the scriptures and teachings.

---

variations on the version I prefer; they refer to the Ox's — not the Boy's — nose, and the visibility of the Ox itself — and not just its tracks.

Following these indications of the Ox's passage, he continues to seek for the Ox itself.

Notice that these tracks are very important. Without them he would not see which direction to follow to the Ox itself. They are signs and indications of reality. Scriptures and tradition, creeds and dogma and doctrines — all work like that. They are all traces leading towards reality. They aren't the reality. They are insubstantial and imperfect. They can only take us up to the gate, which may be either our enlightenment or our encounter with God or possibly our death, but they can't take us through the gate.

The great curse of fundamentalism, which appears in virtually all religions and ideologies, is to mistake the footprints for the animal itself. The instant a scripture or a doctrine or a dogma becomes more than an indication, and in practice becomes an inflexible external standard, the real problems of religion appear. Fundamentalism, both crude (e.g., literalist biblicism) and sophisticated (e.g., medieval and Reformed versions of scholasticism), always flattens spirituality to rote definitions and abstractions. It becomes intolerant in its circular reasoning, imprisoned behind its protective barricades, fearful of sincere questioning and honest doubt, and finally abusive and even murderous.

But the Boy doesn't study the footprints for their own sake. He's not searching for the Ox in order to get, say, an academic degree in Trackology, or to become an adherent of Oxism or Footprintianity. Whatever his formal affiliations might be externally (say, the Rinzai school of Zen Buddhism if a Buddhist, or a Roman Catholic or United

Methodist "school" if a Christian), the Boy's internal search is for the Ox and not for the mere traces of the Ox. Likewise, a true Buddhist's search is not to become outwardly proficient in understanding the Buddha's philosophy in a formal way, but to follow the Buddha's spiritual path to his or her own enlightenment. And, I dare say it, the authentic Christian's search is not to "belong to" any "right-thinking" church or denomination, or to possess some acquaintance with formal dogmas and the Bible, but to follow the spiritual way of Jesus to the kingdom of God.

The footprints, as I've said, are very important for finding the Ox. Scriptures and teachings are very important for finding enlightenment or God. But the tracks are not the Ox, and the scriptures are not substitutes for enlightenment or God. They are not ends in themselves. They won't last forever. Tracks can be washed away by a rainstorm. Tracks can even mislead us if we're not wise in the ways of how to read them with accuracy. Similarly, scriptures are signs; but what we search for is reality, the goal.

The scriptures always should be read, as we journey along, with the lively expectation of the direct experience they indicate. That hope should be uppermost in our minds. The scriptures and teachings we follow denote only, and not even perfectly. The Boy still has his many unanswered questions, which only a transcendent experience will silence with a new kind of clarity: "I still cannot distinguish what is good from what is not; my mind is still confused about truth and untruth." Scriptures and teachings are imperfect traces towards a perfect end.

"But when the perfect comes," writes St. Paul, "the imperfect will pass away" (1 Cor. 13:10).

Meanwhile, towering all the way up to heaven, there in the distance among the faraway mountains, I can see the immensity of the tip of that elusive Ox's *nose*.

3. Seeing the Ox

I hear a nightingale singing cheerfully on a branch.
The sun is warm, a breeze blows soothingly;
*   the willows are green along the riverbank.*
The Ox is standing there all by himself,
*   nowhere to hide.*
That splendid head, those stately horns! —
What artist could portray them?

If I but listen to the everyday sounds, I will come to realiza-
tion and in that moment see the Source. As soon as my
senses are in harmony, they are no different than the true
Source. In all my activities, the Source is manifestly pres-
ent. This union is like salt in water or like color in dye.
When my vision is rightly focused, I find it is not apart
from myself.

The Buddha did not teach that we have no personal
identity, but that our identity changes. In fact, it is
always in a state of fluctuation, and therefore we can't
simply point to ourselves and say, "This is precisely who
I am and who I always will be." Our identities will
change, either without or with our inner awareness and
attention. If it happens without our attention, we find
ourselves in the sort of quandary described in the first
picture — confused, dejected, feeling lost at the junction
of many diverging ways. If the change happens with our

attention rightly focused, we can find the Way and also the Ox.

The Boy represents this changing identity which each of us has. Already the Boy has changed from a fearful and confused to a more focused and settled state of mind. What has altered and ordered his thoughts is finding the "footprints" of the Ox — that is to say, the guidance of the scriptures and teachings. What he has learned to do as a consequence is to focus his mind and attention, to meditate, to listen, to breathe softly like a child, and to allow his senses to experience repose within his own breast. What he has discovered is deep calm in himself, and this harmony within is in accord with the inner heart of living nature.

In Christian terms, the Boy is learning "repentance" *(metanoia)*, which literally means "changing how one thinks." Consider Jesus' first words when he returned to the world from his desert sojourn: "The time is fulfilled, and the kingdom of God is at hand; repent, and believe in the gospel [good news]" (Mark 1:15). A literal rendering of these same words could well be this: "The time is filled to the brim [here and now], and the kingdom of God has drawn near [to you]; be constantly changing your thoughts and constantly trusting in the good message."

This call is for the revision of one's whole life. And one of the principal ways of doing this is to engage in mental prayer or contemplation: "But when you pray [individually], go into your room and shut the door and pray to your Father who is in secret; and your Father who sees in secret will reward you" (Matt. 6:6). As I've noted in earlier books, the Fathers of the church understood "your room" as the room of one's "heart," and "shutting the door" as an invitation to inner concentration. There is little doubt that early Christians practiced forms of meditative interior prayer. Thomas Merton, the great Christian monastic writer, comments somewhere that every religion has a Zen core — and here we can see what he meant.

Jesus' injunction to "shut the door" should not be understood as an admonition to shut the senses to the beauty of creation. It means to shut out distractions — distracting thoughts within and the myriad distracting details without (media, for example, or endless communication, or a constant cycle of business and play). Jesus, as his parables show, was a keen observer of nature. Flowers, birds, fish, growing crops, grazing sheep — the natural world was not lost on him. One can easily surmise that his contemplative life was rich with calm listening and perceiving with his senses. Just as the Boy in the Ten Pictures says that his senses are at one with the Source, so Jesus' senses were one with the Father — the Source — of creation. The "Zen core" of Christianity begins here.

The Boy in the Ten Pictures now sees the Ox. He can see the Ox because his body is relaxed; he is breathing calmly and sitting still. He hears the nightingale singing, notes the greenness of the swaying willows, feels the warmth of the sun and the coolness of a zephyr on his face, and he smells the fragrance of sweet grasses. He could just as easily hear the dripping of rain on a roof or the ticking of a clock, or see the grayness of an overcast sky, or smell the scent of the morning coffee. The point is, he is allowing his senses to sense, and his mind is present and not wandering. He breathes quietly, and if his thoughts stray, he brings them back to his breathing and sensing. In this way he comes to the realization that he is united deeply with the creation immediately around him, and that that which he senses is combined with his senses themselves. It is worth repeating the eloquent words of Kakuan's commentary: "If I but listen to the everyday sounds, I will come to realization and in that moment see the Source. As soon as my senses are in harmony, they are no different than the true Source. In all my activities, the Source is manifestly present. This union is like salt in water or like color in dye. When my vision is rightly focused, I find it is not apart from myself."

The beginning of prayer is stillness and becoming alert to Presence. There is a lovely and evocative passage in Martin Buber's *I and Thou*:

> I contemplate a tree . . .
>
> I can feel it as movement: the flowing veins around the sturdy, striving core, the sucking of the roots, the breathing of the leaves, the infinite commerce with earth and air — and the growing itself in its darkness . . .
>
> But it can also happen, if will and grace are joined, that as I contemplate the tree I am drawn into a relation, and the tree ceases to be an It . . .

> One should not try to dilute the meaning of the re-
> lation: relation is reciprocity . . .[5]

Buber is describing what the Boy in the Ten Pictures ex-
periences: there, in the sensory and contemplative en-
gagement, appears a "You." Buber identifies it as the moment that the "It" becomes to the contemplative eye a
"relation," and the relation, as he says, means that there
is an essential "reciprocity" between the senses and the
thing sensed. A union is established.

For the Boy it is the Ox that is no longer hidden from
him, visible in all its majesty: "The Ox is standing there
all by himself, nowhere to hide./That splendid head,
those stately horns! — /What artist could portray them?"
All at once he is, in other words, aware of the presence he
has been seeking. It has, like the kingdom of heaven,
"drawn near" to him. The reciprocity of this dawning relation lies in the experience that his senses are secretly
and indescribably united to "the Source." Jesus might say
that one has sensed the presence of the "Father who is in
secret."

This is the beginning of contemplative life, the initia-
tion into meditation, a first taste, an initial experience.
But there is still further to go. The Boy will experience
still more in the ongoing transformation of his identity.

5. Martin Buber, *I and Thou,* a new translation with a prologue, "I
and You," and notes by Walter Kaufmann (New York: Charles
Scribner's Sons, 1970), pp. 57-58.

4. Catching the Ox

With the energy of my whole being, I have at last
  taken hold of the Ox!
But how wild his will, how ungovernable his power!
Now he charges up to the highlands, far above
  cloud mists;
And now he is loitering down in some
  impenetrable ravine.

Long time dwelling in the forest, the Ox — but I actually took hold of him today. Long time reveling in these surroundings, he is difficult to control. Longing for sweet-scented grasses, he is still stubborn and refuses to be bridled. If I want the Ox to be tamed, I must apply the whip.

With this particular picture we come back to the question of what the Ox symbolizes. As noted earlier, both the Ox and the Boy are one, the Ten Pictures point to an inner awakening, and — as we shall see — the goal is the uniting of the mind, transcending our selves, and (with the crowning image of Hotei, the Man in the last picture) becoming mature spiritual persons. So, we mustn't think of the Ox as divine (although he potentially has that quality) or profane (although, in this picture, we see that he needs to be tamed, because he can still be unruly). The Ox, like the Boy, is one aspect of the mind.

There are at least two aspects of mind in our selves. The object of meditation is, first of all, to bring the conscious mind to a deeper knowledge of its true nature — we might call it an acknowledging of our subconscious, a realization of our own potent passions, our "dark" and hidden fears, lusts, and sins. The Ox represents that natural, earthy, animal level in our selves every bit as much as it represents our capacity to love and have compassion. The Boy and the Ox must become integrated — the Boy must catch, struggle with, and tame the Ox (even with a whip!) before its true goodness and usefulness can be discovered. The Ox is the Buddha-mind and Buddha-nature, to be sure; but it's also in need of a bridle, some hard taming, and a good scrub-down.

In Christian terms, the Ox isn't simply the kingdom of God, or some sort of symbol of God (even if his nose extends to the heavens!). Rather, he is the most natural part of us, as well as the most "spiritual" — the feeling part of us that can be brought to empathy and stirred to deep involvement with others. In that sense, the Ox, which is united essentially with all created being, is both closest to God in the highest (his heaven-brushing nose again) and at ease in the lowest level of creation. "Now he charges up to the highlands, far above cloud mists;/And now he is loitering down in some impenetrable ravine." He encompasses our spirit and also our passions, our interior heights and depths.

It's wrong to think that Christian spirituality opposes the passions. It seeks instead to discipline them. The passions, or desires, are what move us both to do evil and to do good. Left to themselves, they are unguided, unreasoning potential. They're often chaotic — willful, reactive, sexual, and quite animal. As Aristotle and other Greek philosophers pointed out, the reasoning mind *(nous)* must direct the unreasoning, desiring part of our selves away from straying ("sin" — *hamartia* again), and towards a higher, integrated goal — indeed, towards God, the one who is without parts or passions, the everlasting and almighty Source. It shouldn't surprise us that Christianity, its scriptures written in Greek, used precisely these same terms, adding only that it is by "grace" (meaning a gift of God) that this internal integration of the mind is possible for us at all. The passions, rightly ordered, are invaluable to our lives. Compassion comes from the same interior place as passion, love from the same place as lust, generosity from the same place as greed, self-giving from the same place as selfishness, and so on. The conscious contemplative mind, having "taken hold of the Ox," the undisciplined unconscious and unruly mind, seeks the strength of the Breath of God moving within to tame it.

When the Ox is tamed by the Boy — when the mind's true nature is restored to equilibrium and stability, and the tendency to charge off-course in any direction according to passing whim *(hamartia)* is curbed — then one can say that the kingdom of God has been found.

Lastly, turning to the symbol of "the whip," the immediate thing to note is that it may have direct meaning for Zen Buddhist practice. Often a sharp crack across a practitioner's shoulders from a *keisaku* — a flat wooden stick — wielded by a monk overseeing a meditation session is used to stimulate greater concentration or even sudden self-realization. It's not intended to hurt, but to awaken the mind from potential wandering. The reference to applying "the whip" in Kakuan's commentary may be hinting at that custom.

More generally, of course, the image has to do with "asceticism" — a term which merely means "discipline," such as the discipline of doing physical exercises in order to be fit to compete in sports. Buddhism teaches a middle way between extremes in every aspect of life. In self-discipline, it avoids the extremes of too much laxity on the one hand, and too much exertion on the other. The middle way is the natural way, and it's the best way for the mind to focus on contemplation. One isn't distracted by, say, either a rumbling stomach or a stuffed one. Asceticism in Christianity was originally of such a balanced sort as well. Just as Buddhism avoided ascetical extremes still to be seen in India today (some of them quite sensationalized and grotesque in a carnival-like way), so Christianity avoided the extremes of Greco-Roman paganism. In time, however, harsh forms of asceticism were brought into Christianity by ascetics in an effort to "purify the flesh," and later forms of Christian monasticism (for example, the sixth-century *Rule of St. Benedict*) had to regulate and rectify such overly zealous tendencies. Jesus himself taught no such extremism, and his asceticism consisted of the traditional Jewish practices of prayer, moderate fasting, and almsgiving (cf. Matt. 6). His extended period of fasting in the desert was a special, one-time experience (cf. Matt. 4:1-11; Mark 1:12-13; Luke 4:1-13), just as Buddha's early extreme asceticism was not what he taught during the time of his later mission.

But discipline there must be in the spiritual life. The Boy in the Ten Pictures knows that the Ox must be caught and tamed. Otherwise, he will always go charging off without clear direction, and the consequence will be a sloppy, distracted, unfocused, and scattered mind. Spiritual life will suffer and not progress, and in time it will disappear altogether in mental mists and ravines.

The Ox must be disciplined, and that means applying the whip to our lazy, willful, and stubborn desires. It means learning, in our day and age, to turn off the TV, switch off the cell phone, and get away from the computer; it means learning to eat properly, sleep properly, and pray contemplatively; it means practicing our disciplines of meditation, reading, and silent sitting. And the list could go on. It doesn't mean indulging in ascetical extremes of any sort, especially those of a sickly religious kind (a subject in itself). It means applying those balanced, middle-way practices which really teach us by experience how to keep the passions from straying.

5. Taming the Ox

71

I must hold the nose-rope tight and not let the
 Ox roam,
Else he will wander off down a road of defilements.
Properly trained, he becomes clean and gentle.
Then, untethered, he willingly follows the master.

When one thought arises, another and another follow. Enlightenment turns even this into truth; but if delusion prevails, untruth asserts itself. Delusion originates not in the objective world, but in our own subjective minds. Don't let the nose-rope go slack; hold it tight, and permit no doubt to enter.

The first step of both Buddhist and Christian asceticism is learning to govern one's own thoughts. It is a lifelong discipline, but one that becomes easier over time with vigilance and practice. If sin means going astray and wandering off "down a road of defilements," then we need to be clear that it's our thoughts — how we think — that lead us astray above all else. "Repentance" *(metanoia)*, as I've already mentioned, literally means to *change* (= *meta*) one's own *thoughts* (= *noia*). "Delusion originates not in the objective world, but in our own subjective minds." Taming, or training, the Ox refers to taming our thoughts, our minds, and thus determining the direction our lives will take.

The very first words of the *Dhammapada* are these: "What we are today comes from our thoughts of yesterday, and our present thoughts build our life of tomorrow: our life is the creation of our mind."[6] Everything in Buddhist practice follows from that foundational realization. Similarly, the first words of Jesus are the call to change one's way of thinking and consequent course of life so that the kingdom of God can be received.

The ascetics of Christianity, especially those of the Eastern tradition, knew that the taming of one's thoughts was vital to true discipleship and the following of Jesus' way. Contemplative prayer — stillness, silence, controlled breathing, repetition of a simple biblical phrase or the name of Jesus, and focusing the mind — was employed precisely to master one's thoughts. The literature is vast but accessible, and Christians might do well to seek out editions of *The Philokalia,* or writings of, say, Evagrius of Pontus (the great fourth-century Father of the church) or John Cassian for ancient insights into how one's thoughts can be tamed. Obviously, one must take into account that most of these writings were addressed to monks in a very different age; but, read intelligently, they can be fruitfully used by modern disciples.[7] One should also bear in mind that some of the

6. *The Dhammapada,* translated from the Pali and with an introduction by Juan Mascaró (London: Penguin Books, 1973), 1:5, 12, p. 35.

7. Here are just a few suggestions:

The Philokalia: The Complete Text (in four volumes), compiled by St. Nikodemos of the Holy Mountain and St. Makarios of

asceticism prescribed in these ancient texts would be excessive for many in our age, and a good rule of thumb is the one provided by the twentieth-century spiritual writer Abbot John Chapman: "Pray as you can, not as you can't."[8]

"The science of sciences and art of arts," wrote the fifth-century monk St. Hesychios the Priest, "is the mastery of evil thoughts."[9] This sentence is taken from a treatise on "watchfulness" — that is to say, learning to be watchful of one's own thoughts. The Boy in the Ten Pictures is likewise telling himself to be watchful over the Ox — his own deeper mind, with its feelings and af-

Corinth, translated from the Greek and edited by G. E. H. Palmer, Philip Sherrard, and Kallistos Ware (London: Faber & Faber, 1979-1995).

Early Fathers from the Philokalia (together with some writings of St. Abba Dorotheus, St. Isaac of Syria, and St. Gregory Palamas), translated by E. Kadloubovsky and G. E. H. Palmer (London: Faber & Faber, 1954).

Writings from the Philokalia on Prayer of the Heart, translated by E. Kadloubovsky and G. E. H. Palmer (London: Faber & Faber, 1951).

Evagrius of Pontus: The Greek Ascetic Corpus, translated and with an introduction and commentary by Robert E. Sinkewicz (Oxford: Oxford University Press, 2003).

John Cassian: The Conferences, translated and annotated by Boniface Ramsey, O.P. (Mahwah, N.J.: Newman Press, 1997).

8. Abbot John Chapman's letters of spiritual advice were collected into one volume decades ago, and they still merit reading. See Abbot John Chapman, *Spiritual Letters* (New York/London: Continuum/Burns and Oates, 2004).

9. *The Philokalia,* vol. 1, p. 183.

fections, its desires and neuroses and life's infliction of psychic damage, and its tendency to be deluded and to defile itself with outside enticements — when he speaks of holding the nose-rope tight and not letting doubt enter in.

Discipline, especially at the beginning, requires effort, energy, and mental struggle. It doesn't come easy "just" to sit still and be watchful over one's straying mind. In fact, there's no "just" about it! "Delusion," after all, "originates not in the objective world, but in our own subjective minds." We can be sure that "when one thought arises, another and another follow." Watchfulness will entail effort and intense concentration, particularly when one is starting out on this course.

Watchfulness means that we watch (from above, if you will) the succession of thoughts that emerge (from below, out of our inner depths) while we seek to still the mind. As both Zen masters and Christian ascetics alike have taught, we don't allow our thoughts to carry us along. We let them come and let them go, and just hold tight to our minds so that they don't wander in pursuit. We don't let our delusional thoughts bully us, and we don't chase after them. "Enlightenment," says Kakuan, the Zen master, "turns even this [procession of unruly thoughts] into truth; but if delusion prevails, untruth asserts itself." In other words, by a disciplined watchfulness over the succession of our thoughts (especially those originating in such moods and feelings as anger or bitterness, greed, sexual fantasies and lust, egotism, depression, boredom, and so on) in meditation or contemplative prayer, we see the nature of our unruly selves for what it is. We learn to hold our own mind by the nose-rope and not let it pull loose and wander off after the foolish and hurtful things our subjective desires want to stray after.

St. Hesychios the Priest recommends for Christian disciples five types of watchfulness:

(1) To "scrutinize closely every mental image or provocation." He tells us that by means of mental images, evil thoughts insinuate themselves "into the intellect in order to lead it astray." In our own time this has become a particularly dangerous realm for us to guard ourselves against, since our culture has become largely a visual one. Outside images of sexuality and violence are increasingly difficult to shut out, and their presence in our minds is, to say the least, frequently toxic.

(2) To "free the heart [mind] from all thoughts [or process of thinking], keeping it profoundly silent and still, and in prayer."

(3) To "continually and humbly call upon the Lord Jesus Christ for help." This practice in time would become the Jesus Prayer ("Lord Jesus Christ, have mercy on me"), a helpful repetition in order to keep the mind held tight — like the Boy's use of the nose-rope.

(4) To "have always the thought of death in one's mind." This is perhaps the most important and potent reminder of our impermanence. It was such an exposure to the realities of sickness, old age, and death

that drove the Buddha from his protected, delusional life to seek meaning and truth. To remember death is to keep ourselves face to face with inescapable objective matters, not subjective delusions.

(5) To "fix one's gaze on heaven and to pay no attention to anything material." As a metaphor, this means to look beyond the merely material and to become inwardly open to the transcendent and to God.[10]

These are all disciplines that Christians can put into practice, especially during the time of mental prayer. At other times, our practice of mental prayer should come to direct and shape other areas of our life. In other words, we should not do anything outside of prayer that will undermine our contemplative work, or undo the things we have gained in contemplation. That would be to "let the nose-rope go slack." The Ox is always ready to bolt off again.

However, sometimes we will let go of the Ox's tether, and, when we do, what must we do then? We must go after the Ox immediately and grab hold of that nose-rope — that is to say, return to meditation and watchfulness and those things conducive to discipleship.

I'll conclude this chapter with these words of Evagrius of Pontus, who puts the matter of our contemplation in discipleship boldly, using phrases derived from Jesus himself: "'Go and sell all you have and give to the poor' (Matt. 19:21); and 'deny yourself, taking up your

10. *The Philokalia*, vol. 1, pp. 164-65.

cross' (Matt. 16:24). You will then be free from distraction when you pray. . . . Undistracted prayer is the highest intellection of the intellect."[11]

11. *The Philokalia*, vol. 1, pp. 58-59, 60.

6. *Riding Home on the Ox's Back*

Riding free, I buoyantly wend my way homeward.
Enveloped in the evening mist, the voice of my
*   flute intones.*
Singing a song, beating time, my heart is filled
*   with indescribable joy.*
The Ox requires not a blade of grass.

My struggle is over. Gain and loss no longer concern me. I hum the rustic tune of the woodsman and play the simple songs of the village children. Astride the Ox's back, I serenely gaze at the clouds above. Even if called, no turning back; however enticed, no more disturbance.

Most writings and instructions on the disciplined life necessarily deal with what was described in Picture 5 — the interior struggle and the effort to master one's thoughts and inclinations. This is to be expected; and it's frequently the case that as soon as we think we've achieved self-mastery in some area of our life, we suddenly find the Ox charging off out of control once again and our inner Boy lost in the woods.

But, in fact, the spiritual life often involves more than one of these "pictures" at the same time, and we may find ourselves moving back and forth between them, from one stage to another and back again in cycles. The value of the Ten Ox-Herding Pictures is that they remind us that, no matter where we are or how much ground we may lose at times, we can get back on the path and recover.

We should note that there is nothing grim about these pictures — they are full of humor and have a light touch. Too often we think of discipline and asceticism as cheerless rigor (and we find this all too often, unfortunately, in intense, dour, dull, and gloomy versions of Christian devotion). But the goal of spiritual discipline is not to beat up our selves, or mope about our sins, or tearfully groan about guilt. It is, rather, to find the sort of freedom and joy we see in this picture: "Riding free, I buoyantly wend my way homeward. . . ./Singing a song, beating time, my heart is filled with indescribable joy."

In Christian terms, the state of mind we see in our picture here is described well by the apostle Paul:

For freedom Christ has set us free; stand fast therefore, and do not submit again to a yoke of slavery. . . . But I say, walk by the Spirit, and do not gratify the desires of the flesh. For the desires of the flesh are against the Spirit, and the desires of the Spirit are against the flesh; for these are opposed to each other, to prevent you from doing what you would. But if you are led by the Spirit you are not under the law. . . . The fruit of the Spirit is love, joy, peace, patience, kindness, goodness, faithfulness, gentleness, self-control; against such there is no law. And those who belong to Christ Jesus have crucified the flesh with its passions and desires. (Gal. 5:1, 16-18, 22-24)

The image of crucifixion here is used of something that is past, and in terms of our Ten Pictures it might be said to look back to the inner struggles of our last picture. "Crucifying" unruly "passions and desires" is really no different in our experience than holding tight to the nose-rope of the resistant Ox. "Passions and desires" are the results of delusional thoughts turning us towards "a road of defilements." What we want is freedom from delusion and the enticements of ungoverned thoughts — as Kakuan puts it in our commentary here, what we really want is to be in such a free and joyful state that "even if called [towards pursuing a wrong course, there will be] no turning back; however enticed, [there is] no more [interior] disturbance." This state describes equally the condition of both Boy and Ox, united now and heading home happily together.

Paul describes such a spiritual state of serenity as being in a condition that is free from law ("you are not under the law . . . there is no law"). The Boy had, in the first picture, expressed his anxieties about laws and issues of right and wrong. He saw law in threatening terms: "Ideas of right and wrong come at me like daggers." Law is external, and it weighs on us, sometimes relentlessly inducing nagging feelings of guilt. But the condition of being "in the Spirit [or Breath]" of God is one of interior naturalness and ease. The struggle resolved, contentment and tranquility find a home within. Paul tells us that our inner lives are producing a single fruit made up, perhaps like an orange, of many sections — "love, joy, peace, patience, kindness, goodness, faithfulness, gentleness, self-control." This last segment of the fruit, "self-control," may even serve as the subtitle for this sixth picture. Christians occasionally forget that they are meant to be self-controlled, to possess self-mastery, and that there is nothing at all wrong about becoming self-reliant and self-trusting. "Even if called, no turning back; however enticed, no more disturbance."

But let me stress the words we are meant to stress here. The Boy is "riding *free;*" he is heading home *"buoyantly."* He is *"singing a song, beating time, [his] heart is filled with indescribable joy."* He *"serenely* gaze[s] at the clouds above;" he *"hum[s]* the rustic tune of the woodsman and *play[s] the simple songs* of the village children." In fact, he has become childlike. Whereas, in our first picture, lost in the woods among the maze of intersecting paths, he could say with adult-like anxiety, "Greed for worldly gain and fear of loss spring up like fire," now he says instead: "My struggle is over. Gain and loss no longer concern me." Or, as St. Paul would say, he has "crucified the flesh with its passions and desires." The result of a healthy self-discipline shouldn't be any added mental pain, or taking part in a cult of redemptive suffering, or harboring any haunting fears of future purgative punishments. It should be joyous equanimity and deep satisfaction.

Also to be noted is the increasing effortlessness depicted in the pictures. The nose-rope is gone. "The Ox requires not a blade of grass" — the Ox, in other words, is self-sufficient and content to be ridden by the Boy. After this picture, the Ox will in fact disappear altogether from view. Why is this? Because, as noted from the start, the

Boy and the Ox have always been one and the same. They no longer will need to be depicted as separate entities. With the dawning of "self-control" we see the two "minds" or two aspects of the human mind — the conscious and subconscious, the reasoning self-identity and the super-rational natural mind, the outer self and the true indwelling (Buddha-) nature — conjoined and forming one enlightened, free, self-reliant, and happy person. When this happens, interior relaxation can occur, freedom from confusion and delusion is experienced, and true repose for deepened contemplative experience is born. It is like being reborn, becoming childlike, and one can be simple and straightforward. No more complexities, pretense, or masks.

St. Augustine once described our highest spiritual hope as "no longer being able to sin [wander off]." We could cynically view such a condition as a curtailment of our free choice (and "free choice" is a limited and rather dubious category to begin with). But, whatever Augustine might have meant by that, he didn't mean that we lose freedom when we no longer can wander away in wrong directions or be deluded. Rather, he meant the exact opposite — he meant that we are so free in our selves that we can trust and find rest and not worry about wandering off. Wandering off no longer even interests or entices us.

We can ride the Ox home and look up serenely at the clouds above.

7. Ox Forgotten, Self Alone

Only on the Ox was I able to come home.
But, look — the Ox is now vanished, and serenely
    I sit alone.
Though the red sun rides high in the heavens,
    I placidly dream on.
Under a thatched roof my whip and rope lie idle.

All is one law, not two. The Ox was only a temporary symbol. When a rabbit is caught, a trap is no longer needed; when a fish is caught, a net is no longer needed. It is like gold separated from dross, like the moon breaking through the clouds. One ray of light, serene and penetrating, shines eternally.

Two themes emerge from the poem and commentary for Picture 7: the theme of "home" and the theme of leisure. "Home" in this case is as much metaphorical as it is literal, and leisure means more than just "free time."

First, let's take the subject of "home" and what constitutes a true home for us. When the Boy in the poem says, "Only on the Ox was I able to come home," he is saying something that has an inner meaning. Where is the locale of this home, and why is it that *only* on the Ox could he arrive there?

Taken literally, one of the ideal images of Taoist and Zen spirituality is the lone, retiring hermit seated by his thatched hut in the mountains. This can be, and frequently has been, a sentimentalized picture. Yet the fact remains that not only was it an ideal in the past, but to this very day there are such hermits living in the mountains of China and elsewhere, practicing the Zen life. It may be picturesque to the casual observer, but in reality it is an austere life, though not an impossible one. Unquestionably, it is a rewarding one for many.

Christianity likewise has had a rich tradition of eremitic life. The Desert Fathers lived only marginally more rigorous lives in their caves than they would have done closer to village or city. Daily rural existence in ancient Egypt and Palestine was not an easy one, and most of the Desert Fathers were rustics by background. A city sophisticate and intellectual like the great Evagrius of Pontus was an exception, not the norm. When the Desert Fathers moved out into the wilderness to make their homes there, it wasn't for the sake of making life significantly more difficult than they had already had it back in town or on the farm. They went to remote places for other reasons than testing their endurance.

Stripped of romantic or exaggerated ascetical explanations, the reasons for such retirement, both in the East and the West, have mainly been twofold and related to one another. These are the desire for a simpler, quieter, and more direct contemplative life on the one hand (in fact, for more leisure — even if it means, paradoxically, more leisure in which to struggle); and, connected to this, the desire to get away from what passes for civilization — with its endless cacophony, formal demands, conformity, and phoniness — on the other. At its best, it isn't misanthropy that drives such flight from society, but rather the desire for a more fulfilling and fully *human* existence.

One can pick up the poems and other writings of such great Taoist and Zen figures as Xie Lingyun (385-433 A.D.), Wang Wei (c. 701-761), Hanshan ("Cold Mountain"; ninth century), and Po Chü-i (772-846), and many others through the centuries, to see this ideal expressed movingly.[12] To leave the ersatz and official world behind and to retreat to a simpler life, closer to nature and favorable to deepened attentiveness, is a recurring ideal in both Taoism and Zen Buddhism.

In the West, too, we see the same ideal. Henry David Thoreau is someone who most readily springs to my mind: "I went to the woods," he wrote, "because I wished to live deliberately, to front only the essential facts of life, and see if I could not learn what it had to teach, and not, when I came to die, discover that I had not lived. . . . I wanted to live deep and suck out all the

---

12. A fine little volume of writings (not poems) on this very subject is *Four Huts: Asian Writings on the Simple Life,* translated by Burton Watson and illustrated by Stephen Addis (Boston and London: Shambhala, 1994). It contains four lovely, small descriptive essays by Po Chü-i (817), Yoshishige no Yasutane (982), Kamo no Chōmei (1212), and Matsuo Bashō (1690). Each essay describes the thatched hut each writer built for himself. A key theme that is repeated is that of the public official who leaves behind the demands of office to seek the simple life.

marrow of life. . . . Why should we live with such hurry and waste of life?"[13]

I think as well of Thomas Merton, the influential Trappist monk, who in his last years was given permission to live in a hermitage on the grounds of Gethsemani Abbey in Kentucky. About his home, he wrote this:

This is not a hermitage — it is a house. . . . What I wear is pants. What I do is live. How I pray is breathe. . . . Up here in the woods is seen the New Testament: that is to say, the wind comes through the trees and you breathe it. Is it supposed to be clear? I am not inviting anybody to try it. Or suggesting that one day the message will come saying NOW. That is none of my business.[14]

With these last three sentences he means that the way of life he has found to be "home" for him needn't be how anyone else is called to live. Of Merton, one can say that he was both a Christian monk and a Zen man. Anyone familiar with his fascinating life can see in it a fine example of how the inner "Boy" and the "Ox" merged within him, so that he became, by the time of his early death, something like the Hotei figure we will meet in the last

13. Henry David Thoreau, *Walden* (Rutland, Vt.: Everyman Paperback, 1995), Chapter 1: "Economy."

14. The essay is "Day of a Stranger," and it can be found in numerous collections of Merton's writings. I take this oft-quoted passage now, however, from *Day of a Stranger* by Thomas Merton, introduction by Robert E. Daggy (Salt Lake City: Gibbs M. Smith, Inc., 1981).

of our Ten Pictures. Merton's life was also one of searching for his true home. It is noteworthy that he found it in his own skin at the end. A year before he died in Bangkok, thousands of miles from his Kentucky hermitage, he wrote,

> Life consists in learning to live on one's own, spontaneous, freewheeling: to do this one must recognize what is one's own — be familiar and at home with oneself. This means basically learning who one is, and learning what one has to offer to the contemporary world, and then learning how to make that offering valid.
>
> . . . Hence the paradox that [one's inner identity] finds best when it stops seeking: and the graduate level of learning is when one learns to sit still and be what one has become. . . .[15]

"At home with oneself." With this phrase, Merton touches the very heart of our seventh picture above. He also moves us towards that second theme I mentioned at the outset, that of leisure.

The Boy sits serenely by his thatched-roof hut and dreams placidly. The sun is high and red in the sky, but there he sits in reverie, at home, in leisure. The whip and rope lie useless. The Ox has brought the Boy home — in-

15. Thomas Merton, "Learning to Live," in *Thomas Merton: Spiritual Master*, edited and with an introduction by Lawrence S. Cunningham (Mahwah, N.J.: Paulist Press, 1992), pp. 358, 359.

deed, "only the Ox" could — and now he has vanished altogether as a separate entity. This is because, as the commentary tells us, there is "one law [*dharma*], not two" and just "one ray of light." The "rabbit" and the "fish" have been caught, so the means of catching them have become of no more use. The gold is separated from the dross, and the moonlight has broken free of the obscuring clouds. These miniature parables all point to the same truth: the disciple is free now to relax and merely to be. What needed to be separated has been; what needed to be joined together has been. In Merton's terms, the Boy is "at home with himself" — he can "stop seeking, sit still and be what [he] has become."

"Home" is basically wherever we can find our leisure and be the integrated selves we have become. This may come after many years, or as a flash of enlightenment at an early age. Whenever in life it shows up, it lies only on the other side of confusion, searching, struggle, self-discipline, and finding our true mind. It is the repose after inner work, and not accessible without inner work. It is the stage of contemplation in which we find that we can accept our selves as they are, warts and all. We aren't "perfect," but we know where we're headed and who we are, and we know that wandering off ox-like is now very unlikely (though watchfulness is still something we practice, naturally and habitually now). Our home is in our skin, and our thatched-roof hut is our own head.

In Christian terms, we no longer have any fear of God — "perfect love casts out all fear" of him (1 John 4:18). We will pursue the subject of union with God in the discussion of our next picture, but here we only comment that we have — like the prodigal son — returned to our father's home, and now we can "find rest for our souls" (cf. Matt. 11:29).

Leisure is not something we allow ourselves only after we have done all of our daily, worldly duties. It isn't laziness or sacking out after a hard day's routine. Leisure may look useless in our workaholic and play-aholic world, but it isn't measured by "usefulness." In fact, it's not a "thing" to be measured at all, but the way of simply and reflectively being. It should become central to our lives. Everything else said to be useful to us is really only useful when it allows us meditative leisure, or even the freedom for reverie — that is to say, when it allows us to be genuinely ourselves.

Leisure should be our primary spiritual duty for our own sakes; I mean, of course, the leisure of contemplation — stillness, silence, and being in God's presence. In leisure we read the scriptures, as Picture 2 mentioned; in leisure we see the Ox, as Picture 3 revealed; in leisure, we struggle to catch him and tame him, as in Pictures 4 and 5; and in leisure, we find that we can recline on the Ox's back and let him take us home, as in Picture 6. Finally, we find the Ox has taken up residence within us, and we find ourselves more free and natural and untroubled ("spontaneous, freewheeling"). And then our leisure becomes something we have at the very base of all the other areas of our life.

This settledness and interior stability, which are the fruits of contemplative leisure, are usually associated with age, and even more with wisdom. And one of the goals of our lives is to find our home in our own acquired wisdom.

Only the Ox could bring us to that home in the end, and that home always proves to be anywhere and every-where, wherever we may be.

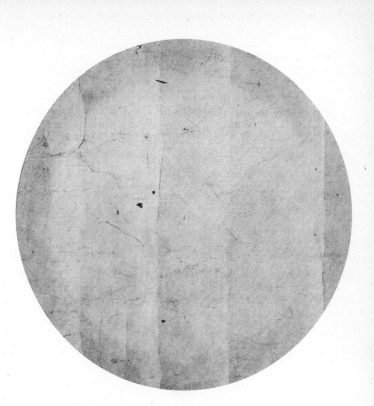

8. Both Ox and Self Transcended

All is empty — whip, rope, person, Ox.
Who can ever appraise heaven's immeasurable
vastness?
Over a burning fire no snowflake can last.
When this state of mind is realized, the spirit
of the ancient masters is manifest.

All confusion has perished; serenity prevails; even the idea of "holiness" has vanished. I linger not with the thought of Buddhahood achieved, and I go quickly past the thought of Buddhahood not achieved. Since I stay in neither condition of mind, not even a thousand eyes could discern my specific quality. If hundreds of birds were now to strew my path with flowers, such homage would be farcical.

Pictures 7, 8, 9, and 10 are all aspects of the same mature state of mind, looked at from the perspectives of four essential relationships as affected by spiritual awakening. Picture 7, as we saw, indicated peace with oneself (at "home" inwardly, in a position of contented leisure). Pictures 9 and 10 will show us right relationships with the world of nature and the world of human society respectively. Now, with Picture 8, we turn to harmony with the ultimate (the state of *nirvāna*), the infinite, the Tao, or — in the terms best understood in Christianity — with God.

It is represented here by an empty circle. I believe this is so for two reasons. I will take these one at a time.

First, the empty circle reminds us that to depict or define the ultimate or God is not possible. "God is an infinite sphere," it has been written, quoted, and re-quoted down the centuries, "whose center is everywhere, and whose circumference is nowhere." In other words, one must either depict God as including and transcending everything (an impossibility), or else give up any attempt at adequate representation entirely. The empty circle in Picture 8 does the latter. It literally depicts nothing, but that nothing is everything and boundlessly more. In the words of the *Tao Te Ching*,

> Tao is empty
>> yet it fills every vessel with endless supply
> Tao is hidden
>> yet it shines in every corner of the universe . . .
>
> So deep, so pure, so still
>> It has been this way forever . . .[16]

Turning back to Christianity, we don't think of God in such impersonal terms, but we do think of him in super-personal terms. He is more than "personal" in Christian theology. The three "Persons" (an inadequate term if ever there was one) of the Trinity are not *human* or *created* persons. We use the word "person" in this case

16. *Tao Te Ching*, verse 19, p. 5.

only advisedly and analogically. In fact, we use all language and all concepts about God in this way — God transcends infinitely every analogy or notion we have concerning him. We call this way of reasoning about the divine the "negative way" *(via negativa)* or "apophatic" theology (from the Greek word *apophemi,* meaning "to deny" something — in this sense, "to deny" that God is really "like" any of our conceptions, even our most cherished and hallowed ones!).

The most orthodox Fathers and mystics of the church have always insisted on this. Language about God can never be literal. We are always bound to use analogies to refer to him. The poet Rainer Maria Rilke was only echoing what Christian theologians have taught for centuries when he wrote somewhere that "God is the direction and not the object of love." God cannot be an "object" among other objects. As uncreated being, he is outside every frame of reference we have. St. John of Damascus put the matter succinctly, writing in the eighth century that God "is infinite and incomprehensible, and all that is comprehensible about him is his infinity and incomprehensibility."[17]

Vladimir Lossky, the Russian Orthodox theologian, went so far as to write, "Apophaticism teaches us to see above all a negative meaning in the dogmas of the Church; it forbids us to follow natural ways of thought

17. Quoted in Vladimir Lossky, *The Mystical Theology of the Eastern Church* (Cambridge and London: James Clarke & Co. Ltd., 1957), p. 36.

and to form concepts which would usurp the place of spiritual realities. For Christianity is not a philosophical school for speculating about abstract concepts, but is essentially a communion with the living God."[18] Meister Eckhart, the thirteenth-century mystical theologian, went even further than that when he counseled that in the deepest contemplation all concepts of "God" must be abandoned:

> The soul must exist in a free nothingness. That we should forsake God [meaning our ideas about God] is altogether what God intends, for as long as the soul has God, knows God, and is aware of God, she is far from God. This then is God's desire — that God should reduce himself to nothing in the soul so that the soul may lose herself. For the fact that God is called God comes from creatures. . . . This is the greatest honor that the soul can pay to God, to leave God to himself and to be free of him.[19]

"Free nothingness" brings us rather close to the image of the empty circle in Picture 8, and to the words of Kakuan's poem: "Who can ever appraise heaven's immeasurable vastness?/Over a burning fire no snowflake [in context, no limited human concept of heaven's vastness]

---

18. Lossky, *The Mystical Theology of the Eastern Church*, p. 42.

19. *Meister Eckhart: Selected Writings*, selected and translated by Oliver Davies (London: Penguin Books, 1994), sermon 30, "Selected German Sermons," pp. 244-45.

can last./When this [contemplative] state of mind is realized, the spirit of the ancient masters is manifest." That
this realization is also, as Lossky says, "a communion
with the living God" is something that we can discover
only by experiencing it for ourselves.

The second reason for using the image of the empty
circle in Picture 8 is that it points the viewer not only towards an apophatic understanding of the transcendent
One, but also towards the effects that our union with that
reality has on our character and aspirations. As the first
line of our poem says, "All is empty — whip, rope, person, Ox." "Empty" in this instance means "forgotten,"
which is to say that these things and what they represent
have vanished from our thoughts and active consider-
ations. In the presence of God, everything else recedes
from view.

Using the Zen Buddhist terminology of our pictures,
even the idea that one has or has not achieved "Buddhahood" is meaningless. What difference do concepts make
now? The old doctrinal indicators and ascetical routines
can, and should, be left behind, at least as long as the encounter with reality — with God — lasts.

Such moments come and go in contemplation, of
course, but they have lasting effects. Not the least effect is
the dawning perspective that all the signposts — the concepts, dogmas, doctrines, systems, creeds, scriptures, and
so on — that got us to this point are only relative to the ex-
periential destination. It isn't blasphemy to say that "even
the idea of 'holiness' has vanished," or that "if hundreds
of birds [Christians might say "angels"] were now to strew

my path with flowers, such homage would be farcical." It isn't blasphemy or flippancy; it's the naturalness of humility, or the humility of naturalness — this is what really should be normal, everyday stuff, and not the object of awe and reverence. "Sainthood," in other words, is supposed to be an ordinary, natural, easygoing condition, not special, and definitely not seen as anything sensational: "Not even a thousand eyes could discern my specific quality." (This will be taken up again in Picture 10, of course, with the beaming, bare-chested, wine-bearing figure of Hotei.) Here I'm reminded, though, of the hard-to-grasp nature of the enlightened follower of Jesus in the eyes of others: "The wind blows where it wills, and you hear the sound of it, but you do not know whence it comes or whither it goes; so it is with every one who is born of the Spirit" (John 3:8).

The empty circle is the picture that once crowned the Ox-Herding Pictures. One can understand why; but Kakuan wasn't satisfied with it. Beyond the attainment of enlightenment and Buddhahood, and beyond contemplative union with God, there remain our relationships to nature and to other human beings. Kakuan added Pictures 9 and 10 to force us to look further than ourselves and our own spiritual attainments to the greater world. In so doing, the Christian may be reminded of this key insight: "He who does not love does not know God; for God is love" (1 John 4:8). It appears that Kakuan, in his own Zen Buddhist way, would agree with that sentiment.

9. *Returning to the Origin, Back to the Source*

Too many steps have been taken in vain, returning
    to the Origin, coming back to the Source.
Better to have been blind and deaf from
    the beginning.
Sitting in my hut, I am unconcerned about
    things outside.
Streams flow on of themselves, and the flowers
    are red.

From the beginning pure, I have not been affected by defilement. I observe the forms of integration and disintegration, but I abide in the unshakable serenity of non-assertion. I do not become attached to the changes. Why then is there need to strive for anything? The waters are blue, the mountains are green. Sitting alone, I observe things endlessly changing.

I f in our last picture we were presented with an empty circle, in this picture we are presented with an image of twisting, curling, living nature. The very twists and turns of the roots, the blossoms budding on the tree limbs, the suggestion of swirling mists or eddies of a stream beyond — all suggest the "endlessly changing" nature of nature. "Streams flow on of themselves, and the flowers are red." "The waters are blue, the mountains are green." The disciple observes "the forms of integration and disintegration," but he is not "attached to the changes." Serenely, he has come to accept the transient nature of everything, even the impermanence that so troubled the young Shakyamuni Buddha.

Impermanence is a cause of suffering. We try to hold on to things and to people, to places and times, to life and health, to our vocation and our relationships — but these things keep moving and changing. Times change, people die, and the very landscapes we cherish in memory are not constant. Impermanence creates in us the desire for permanence — we don't want to suffer, we don't want to see or participate in the inevitabilities of illness, aging, and death. We hold on, become attached, don't want to let go. And yet, it is the nature of nature that we can't hold on to anything, and finally must let go of everything — even of our selves. One of the Buddha's Four Noble Truths is that suffering ceases when attachment to our desires ceases. Our desires are always somehow connected to our deep discomfort with impermanence and change.

What the disciple in Picture 9 has discovered is that stability in the midst of impermanence is possible, and that it has always been a potential within him. Looking back over his previous confusion and chasing after the Ox, he can now say — rather startlingly — "Too many steps have been taken in vain, returning to the Origin, coming back to the Source./Better to have been blind and deaf from the beginning."

What does he mean by this? Does he mean to say that his entire journey from and to home has been in vain? It reminds one of the conclusion of the film version of *The Wizard of Oz*, when Dorothy answers the question about what it is she has learned from her journey to Oz with the rather unsatisfying declaration that "There's no place like home." Well, yes, indeed that is what the disciple is saying too. In fact, he seems to maintain, he should have remained "blind and deaf" to all the enticements that led him from his true home. Why did he ever need to "return" to the Origin and "come back" to the Source? Why did he ever leave in the first place (a question we could all ask ourselves)?

Even more alarming — perhaps especially to a Western Christian's ears, with peculiar notions of having been conceived in sin ("original sin") possibly churning between them — is the disciple's claim about himself: "From the beginning pure, I have not been affected by defilement." What does he mean by this?

We must recall that in the East there is no idea of original sin. Not even in Eastern Christianity is there such a notion. No one is born "depraved" or guilty of the sins of the race. What is meant here is certainly not a denial that the disciple has gone off-course (the literal meaning of "sin" — *hamartia* — as you may recall), which is something that all have done; but rather that underneath all the confusion and dirt and struggle involved in his having gone off-course, deep down within himself there always remained that which was essentially pure and undefiled. A Christian might well call this pure center of the self "the image of God" within, which is never lost but only obscured by our sinfulness; and even after the worst that sin can do to us, it can be restored and made pure again. Being "born again" means precisely that.

Coming to terms with impermanence, then, is as much a matter for the Christian's discipleship as it is for the Buddhist's. Finding the inner serenity and permanent stability that non-attachment affords us is vital. Like the disciple of our Ten Pictures, we must learn to "abide in the unshakable serenity of non-assertion," "unconcerned about things outside" (meaning those things that will change, regardless of how much one might have a "concern" to prevent that), not "attached to the changes," and not striving against them. The justly famous "Serenity Prayer" comes to mind as apt here: "God, grant me the serenity to accept the things I cannot change, courage to change the things I can, and wisdom to know the difference." Some things we can change (the story of the Ten Pictures has been all about such change), but there are countless things we can't. The nature of nature — the endless changes and cycles that manifest the living Source and Origin at work — we cannot change. But we can observe.

We shouldn't miss the point that, although the disciple sits in his hut "unconcerned about things outside," he nonetheless *observes*. What does he observe? "I observe," he says, "the [natural] forms of integration and disintegration." He also observes, as we've seen, that "streams flow on of themselves, and the flowers are red," and that "the waters are blue, the mountains are green." Again, please note that he *observes* them; he doesn't ig-

nore them. In his newfound acceptance of impermanence, aware of his own abiding inner stability (the foun-
dation of which we have discussed with Picture 8), he is
now free to delight in the nature of nature as never before. He can just let it be itself, as he can let himself be
and let God be. He has learned non-attachment, non-
assertion, and non-striving. He needn't qualify or quan-
tify what he observes so much as take it as it comes.
There's a time for measuring and using the resources of
nature, but this time of leisured contemplation isn't that
time. Before one uses it rightly and respectfully, one
must first appreciate it. *One must learn to forgo the false
"need" to control.*

As Picture 8 pointed us to the Christian idea of
apophaticism, Picture 9 points us to the complementary
approach to God that we call the *via positiva* or "kata-
phaticism." The latter is a big word that means, simply,
"to affirm." In this case, it means "to affirm" that the hidden God can be spoken about, concepts about God can be
valuable (even concepts expressed in pictures of empty
circles), all is not mere silence, and — most importantly
— everything that exists materially and sensually indicates his living reality.

But it isn't simply a matter of "seeing God in nature"
in some poetic or allegorical sense; rather, it's a matter of
waking up and discovering nature in God. All forms are
of themselves empty — made of nothing — but God is
what ceaselessly makes them to be. He imagines them
forth, and we receptively imagine them in. God isn't "in"
nature; we can of course see nature — as many do — and

not see him in it at all. But once there has been a deep experience of enlightenment, as Picture 8 suggests, we find that nature and its perpetual transformations endlessly flow from that indefinable Source which Christians and others call God. We can no longer see nature and not see the Source behind it. "Too many steps have been taken in vain, returning to the Origin, coming back to the Source" — that is to say, it should have been obvious to us from the start.

For Christians, of course, the greatest "affirmation" of nature is that "the Word" (an abstract concept of a transcendent reality) "became flesh" in Jesus Christ (John 1:1, 14) — "flesh" being nothing if not a natural, material, sensual substance. By affirming this, Christians affirm the essential goodness of the nature of nature. We can observe it, love it, and be thankful for it; but — like the Buddhist — we must accept the fact that all things "flow on of themselves" and are "endlessly changing."

Impermanence is how things are, and in serenity and peaceful observation we need have no fear of it. Even death loses its sting when we recognize it as the natural way of things. We might likewise think of the Resurrection in such terms as well. Indeed, St. Paul suggests this very thing with his completely naturalistic analogy: "What you sow does not come to life unless it dies. And what you sow is not the body which is to be, but a bare kernel, perhaps of wheat or of some other grain. . . . So is it with the resurrection of the dead" (1 Cor. 15:36-37, 42).

When we relate to the natural world with such detachment and appreciative attention, not asking too many un-answerable questions, accepting that the ways of nature are God's concern and not ours; when we recognize that we should only use nature's resources sparingly and as in-trinsically sacred, and, insofar as it is possible, protect na-ture's right to exist just as it is without too much control or unnecessary interference, then we will find peace with it. Human civilization has had an increasingly poor rela-tionship with the natural creation over the past few centu-ries. Our mishandling of the earth and its resources is a story of abuse and addiction, and the lamentable mess we've made of things is catching up with us. The tough answers to this situation, as in every aspect of our exis-tence, lie in the disciplines we find among our spiritual roots, in those great sources of wisdom we have left behind.

The crisis with which we are faced requires that the Boy get out of his spiritual confusion and find the Ox and return home to the Origin. Primarily, as we have ex-plored here, that is an individual necessity, a personal quest. But it is also a collective necessity and quest. Ei-ther we will discover as a civilization how to live simply, more deeply, in harmony with nature's ways (which are God's ways), or else we will find that a good and natural impermanence has turned instead to our own final dev-astation.

10. *Entering the Marketplace with Bliss-Bestowing Hands*

Bare-chested and barefooted, I enter
　　the marketplace.
Muddied and dusty, how broadly I grin.
I have no recourse to magical powers.
Now, before me, withered trees burst into bloom.

The gate of my hut is closed, and even the wisest do not know me. No glimpses of my inner life are seen. I go my own way, making no attempt to follow the steps of ancient sages. Carrying my wine gourd, I go out into the marketplace; I return home, leaning on my staff. I am found in the company of winebibbers and fishmongers, and they all become enlightened.

When I read this, I am reminded of passages such as these:

And as he sat at table in the house, behold, many tax collectors and sinners came and sat down with Jesus and his disciples. And when the Pharisees saw this, they said to his disciples, "Why does your teacher eat with tax collectors and sinners?" But when [Jesus] heard it, he said, "Those who are well have no need of a physician, but those who are sick. Go and learn what this means, 'I desire mercy, and not sacrifice.' For I came not to call the righteous, but sinners." (Matt. 9:10-13)

> "The Son of man came eating and drinking, and [the self-righteous] say, 'Behold, a glutton and a drunkard, a friend of tax collectors and sinners!' Yet wisdom is justified by her deeds." (Matt. 11:19)

The model that Jesus set before his disciples was that of one so inwardly free and self-assured that he can mingle in the marketplace, eat and drink and be sociable, and yet have the ability to gather around him a community of those who seek the kingdom of God. His methods were considered scandalous by the religious elite of his day, and his message novel and not in accord with the "ancient sages" of his people. He had the audacity, in the minds of some, to interpret the Law of God in ways that seemed to undermine its godly severity — always he emphasized mercy, healing, forgiveness, and new life. "I came that they may have life, and have it abundantly. I am the good shepherd. The good shepherd lays down his life for the sheep" (John 10:10-11).

When we reach Picture 10, we reach what is, in Kakuan's eyes, the true way of the enlightened disciple. He is to be a *bodhisattva* — one who leaves his own gate closed behind him and journeys through the mud and dust of the defiling world into the social world of daily human life. "A bodhisattva resolves: I take upon myself the burden of all suffering, I am resolved to do so, I will endure it. I do not turn or run away, do not tremble, am not terrified, nor afraid, do not turn back or despond. . . . In that I do not follow my own inclinations. I have made the vow to save all beings. All beings I must set free."[20] Hotei, as we saw earlier, was such a bodhi-sattva. We have already described this beaming, joyful figure at length. It is enough to note here that he is a symbol, among other things, of "abundant life" and *good* news. His broad grin is a reminder that the way of enlightenment is not sour or dour — it is, after all, a satisfied *life*.

Many versions of this last picture depict only the corpulent, jolly Hotei, grasping a staff, his enormous sack of good things thrown casually over one shoulder, a wine gourd in his hand. This version depicts Hotei with another figure. Since it is said to be based directly on Kakuan's original picture, we can believe that that also had this second character in it. Hotei, as we said in an earlier chapter, is a symbol — in fact, he is yet another symbol for the same disciple symbolized by the Boy and also the Ox, but now enlightened, mature, and the embodiment of the generous, gift-giving, self-giving, bliss-bestowing bodhisattva. Who, then, is this second figure? It is quite clearly *the Boy!*

Or, is it? I have wondered about this for far too many hours, and I can understand why later artists of the pictures simply left this confusing detail out. Still, if Kakuan put the Boy in the original, I'm at pains to understand why. Two possibilities occur to me. Either it is the same

20. *The Teachings of the Compassionate Buddha*, edited, with commentary, by E. A. Burtt (New York: New American Library, 1955), p. 133.

Boy contemplating his future, ripened self, or it is another Boy entirely.

If the first option is adopted, then we have a kind of
cycle suggested — the Boy contemplating Hotei's image
inside the picture is meant to represent the real-life "Boy"
(i.e., disciple) who is looking at the Ten Pictures and contemplating them *outside the picture:* it is *us,* in other
words — we who are at the very moment gazing at the
Ten Pictures. Inside the picture he stands and contemplates what he aims to become (Hotei, an enlightened
one, a bodhisattva), while outside the picture the flesh-
and-blood disciple contemplates the whole scroll and
range of pictures. I like this interpretation, and it has a
gentle, good-natured humor about it.

The second option is not all that different from the
first. The Boy, according to this interpretation, is another
disciple entirely. He looks exactly like the Boy of previous
pictures because all disciples start at the same immature
level. The Boy is then the depiction of a state of mind —
the state of mind that must soon go looking for the
Buddha-mind, the Ox. He looks at Hotei, and like the
winebibbers and fishmongers in the commentary who
are attracted to the ebullient bodhisattva, he is setting out
on the road to enlightenment.

But it is the Hotei figure who is the real focus in Picture 10, and some further comments about him are necessary. We have noted similarities with Christ, but we
need to take another step and remind ourselves that the
enlightened disciple in the poem and commentary, far
from giving the impression of being just a "follower,"

praises his "own way": "I go my own way, making no attempt to follow the steps of ancient sages." He is more than a follower now; he has become someone who walks with conscious self-possession.

This is no Sinatra-style, "I did it my way" willfulness, however. In fact, there is no longer any ego absorption involved at all. What is described is the inner stability we have looked at so closely in earlier pictures. It is the naturalness, the ordinariness of holiness. "I have no recourse to magical powers," he says. There is nothing outwardly remarkable about him, no sensationalism, no self-advertising. "The gate of my hut is closed, and even the wisest do not know me. No glimpses of my inner life are seen." All they see is a broad grin, the dust of real life on his clothes, sociability, joy, and the sort of casual nature that allows for a bit of drinking and conversation. He is obviously someone who is flexible, self-controlled, and self-reliant, not rigid or censorious. There is no smell of cant or religiosity about him, he's not sanctimonious, and he doesn't speak in pious jargon. He takes the world as he finds it, doesn't recoil from it or the people who live in it, knowing that he has no desire for its stuff or fear that it can really defile him anymore. He doesn't foolishly presume this to be the case. He has passed through the rigors of discipleship under a teacher, and he knows himself well enough to have assurance. People find him approachable, relaxed, and interesting. Like Jesus, he is just fine eating with sinners — and even tax collectors! Like Jesus at the wedding of Cana, he might even provide the wine. And yet, he is there with a message of salvation and enlightenment: "I am found in the company of winebibbers and fishmongers, and they all become enlightened." He comes "that they may have life, and have it abundantly": "Now, before me, withered trees burst into bloom."

For the follower of Jesus, this sort of natural self-reliance should also be an ideal. Too often it isn't. But each one of us has his or her place and time and circle of relationships. None of us follows Jesus in such a way that we become cookie-cutter look-alikes. None of us prays each other's prayers or possesses each other's faith. None of us should feel ourselves so dependent on grace that we wouldn't trust ourselves not to fall into debauchery at the first opportunity. That stage is the one we see in our first picture — no one is meant to be stuck there. There are nine more stages to go! We must all learn, going along the individual spiritual inner paths we must take, how to be who we really are, how to know God as he is in our interior experience, how to relate to the natural world as a revelation, and how to mingle in the social world without fear or hypocrisy, but with love and empathy. We should together become a community of Christian bodhisattvas, disciples who support both the commonality and the personal diversity of discipleship.

The Ten Ox-Herding Pictures remind us of the perennial wisdom to be found in all the world's great spiritual traditions. Christians can look at the Boy, the Ox, and Hotei as a depiction of the disciple's path. We can see, if we have eyes to see, the figure of the Good Shepherd behind that of the Ox-Herder.

Jesus is never far wherever truth is found.

Christ the Good Shepherd,
Catacomb of San Callisto, Rome

Scala / Art Resource, NY